# INSIDE IRAN

Paul Hunt

A LION PAPERBACK

Published by
**Lion Publishing**
Icknield Way, Tring, Herts, England
ISBN 0 85648 378 8
**Albatross Books**
PO Box 320, Sutherland, NSW 2232, Australia
ISBN 0 86760 297 X

First edition 1981



The photographs in this book are reproduced by kind permission of:
The Rev. Dick Ashton, page 133
Associated Newspapers, pages 6, 115
Church Missionary Society, page 80
The author, pages 25, 43, 61, 97, 152

Printed and bound in Great Britain by
Richard Clay (The Chaucer Press) Ltd, Bungay, Suffolk

TSI
125

**Inside Iran**



The echoes of the Iranian revolution are still heard round the world. It is a classic confrontation - traditional against modern, East against West. Different value-systems face each other in conflict.

But what was it like to be there? This book is a first-hand account, written by someone who was in Teheran right up to the last possible moment.

Paul Hunt was chaplain to the Bishop of Iran. During six years in Iran he learnt to love the country deeply. Then came those final months, in which he narrowly escaped assassination, saw other Christians imprisoned or killed, and tried to sustain friendships with Iranian Muslims developed over the years.

This is a book about *what* happened, but it also tries to understand *why* it happened. It never strays beyond what the writer experienced for himself. The focus throughout is on *people* - not the famous names, but ordinary men and women struggling to come to terms with a totally new situation.

Paul Hunt worked with parishes in Britain and with students in Malaysia, before going to Iran in 1974. He is married, with two daughters.

To Diana,
who has shared with me in the experiences of this book

# Contents

Safely back in Britain, Paul and Diana Hunt, with Rosemary, born in Britain during home leave, and Deborah, born at their home in Isfahan just after the Christian hospital had been seized.

# 1
# MAYDAY

It was nine o'clock in the morning on Thursday 1 May 1980. I bent over the blood-soaked body of our friend and neighbour Jean Waddell, secretary to the Bishop of Iran. She lay on her bed in the apartment immediately above our own. At that moment I felt she had only minutes to live.

'Can you hear me, Jean?' I pressed her hand to let her know it was me.

She nodded.

I knew how vital it was to get her to tell me who her assailants were and why she had been shot. Considering she was drifting in and out of consciousness, her answers were remarkably clear.

'Two young men with guns . . . they asked for you . . . for Paul Hunt . . . asked if I was your wife . . . where you were . . . told them you were our pastor . . . lived downstairs with your wife and two small children . . .'

It's hard to say how I felt just then. A kind of emptiness filled me. It was a hot summer morning in the heart of Teheran, but the sweat on my face was cold.

'It could just as easily have been me lying on that bed,' I kept saying to myself. 'If it was me they were looking for, why didn't they find me?'

The police were all around us. I held Jean's hand and tried my utmost to reassure her. Her feet had been tied with stockings and she had obviously been violently beaten. I wondered if she would live. It seemed the ambulance would never come. Three-quarters of an hour was an eternity. They telephoned yet again.

Never was the sound of a siren more welcome. Four of us lifted her down the three flights of stairs, leaving a trail of blood. Jean's groans became mine as I held her swaying body in the ambulance. Would we get there in time to save her?

## Alone and defenceless

It was some hours before we could be clear what had happened in Jean's apartment – and how it came about that we found her in time. Later that day I sat with my wife, Diana, and we began to put together the pieces of the jigsaw.

The two gunmen had entered the three-storey building at about 8.30 in the morning. They must have climbed over the wall (not a difficult thing to do) and somehow forced the lock on the ground-floor door. They had chosen just the right day. The streets of Teheran were full of millions of people marching on the May Day parade – 'Workers of the World unite!' No-one would trouble to interfere. They could get in, commit the planned murder and escape unseen.

They went up the stairs, for some reason going straight past our flat on the first floor. Then they waited at Jean's door and, when she opened it to go into the kitchen outside her small apartment, they pointed revolvers at her and forced her back in. For about half an hour there was no violence. One of them sat down and the other moved round the room picking up different things and asking her about them – including her work permit. They asked questions, mainly about me. She even offered them a cup of tea, but they refused.

Eventually they told her the building was surrounded by revolutionary guards and she must be blindfolded and taken to the 'revolutionary garden' (no-one has ever heard of such a place). Jean said there was no need to blindfold her. She was alone and defenceless and would happily go with them.

Later she described what happened.

'They decided to use a blouse of mine as a blindfold. One of them went behind me, but instead of blindfolding me he hooked his left arm round my neck and jerked me off my feet. The other one grabbed my feet and it seemed they were beating my body, concentrating on my stomach. It was like an explosion of violence and I felt they were trying to break my neck or strangle me. I struggled for air. It was very painful but fortunately I passed out quickly.

'Some time later I woke up in my bed bathed in sweat and thinking "Gosh that was a nightmare; thank goodness I have woken up". Then I realized I couldn't move my limbs. My hands were tied to my sides with the blouse they had wanted to blindfold me with and my feet were tied with a pair of stockings. I was very hot. After what seemed an age I managed to free my hands and then untie my feet. I threw the quilt off and managed to sit up, hoping to reach the desk where the phone was. My left side was very heavy but I didn't then realize that I'd been shot. They must have done that while I was lying unconscious. I fell back on the bed and groaned a great deal . . .'

## No picnic

While this was happening we were in our flat downstairs, eating breakfast on our day off. We had decided the night before to go for a picnic and invite Jean to join us. As always with two small children it was a noisy breakfast. So we heard nothing of the drama going on upstairs. Rosemary, our three-year-old, had a very special friendship with Jean and would often go up to see her and they would go shopping together. She insisted on going with Diana to ask Jean out. I wanted a bit of peace and quiet so they took our one-year-old, Deborah, with them. There was no answer when they knocked and

Diana was about to turn away thinking Jean had gone shopping. But, true to form, Rosemary was not to be deterred. She went on banging and banging.

'Surely Jean wouldn't go shopping without me. She's got to answer the door.'

Suddenly the door was opened, but not by Jean. Two young men pointed revolvers at them. They were, Diana thought, rather nervous and undecided what to do. They looked about them and then put Diana in the bathroom with the children, telling her if she didn't make a sound, they would let her out later. As Diana reflected: 'When you're holding on to two kids you don't argue with armed men.'

My wife sat in the bathroom trying hard to keep the children happy playing with the water. She was fighting to keep her mind clear. She felt numb, hoping and praying that I wouldn't decide to come upstairs, as they would probably shoot me. She wondered what on earth had happened to Jean. And what might they do when they let her out?

## Spot-on timing

Later, looking back on the whole drama, we realized how absolutely extraordinary it was that Diana went up at that precise time and took the children with her. We looked at the might-have-beens. If she had gone up five minutes later it is likely the gunmen would have shot Jean again and killed her (they obviously intended this). Or if they had left the flat, locking the inner door (as they later did), Diana would have assumed Jean was out and our friend would have died within two hours from loss of blood. The surgeon at the hospital said she only had an hour to live when he operated on her.

Again, since they had heard from Jean that we lived below, and it was me they were searching for, they might well have come to find me. Or if I had gone up on my own to find Jean they would almost certainly have shot me. As it is, all Iranians love children and would never want to harm them. Diana, a defenceless woman, didn't cause the same kind of threat to them. And so it was by Diana choosing that precise time to go up that Jean's life was saved, and our lives were left intact.

They stayed in that bathroom for half an hour. It seemed much longer. Rosemary and Deborah became restless and started to cry. Diana opened the door a fraction and saw to her surprise that the outer door leading to the stairs was open. She didn't know where the gunmen were but decided to pick up both children and get down those stairs as fast as possible. Too scared to come into our flat on her way down (what nameless horror might have happened there?), she made it to the street. There were no other foreigners living near to us, but our Iranian neighbours came up trumps. They immediately invited her and the children into their home and phoned the police. This family gave them sweets, oranges and cucumbers (eaten as a fruit in Iran). They gave dolls to Rosemary and even a bottle to Deborah. Diana had to refuse when they wanted her to stay all day, but she explained someone must find out where I was. Other neighbours rang the outside bell to our flat, and I came into the street, quite unaware that anything was amiss.

In a few terse sentences Diana explained what had happened. The street was now filling with people. Two men took me into the apartment to see if there were explosives in the cellar beneath. The police arrived and immediately fired shots through the window of Jean's flat. We didn't know if the gunmen were still there. They wanted me to go upstairs with them, but as I was unarmed, discretion prevailed and I waited below. Then they called me to join them as they knocked down the locked door of Jean's flat. Jean described it to us later:

'. . . in one of my lucid moments it was a wonderful sight to see the outside door of my flat splinter under the boots of a large Iranian policeman who simply walked through it followed by Paul Hunt . . . and I heard Paul's voice saying "Jean".'

## Coincidences happen

When we arrived at the hospital we learned that a highly qualified French-trained surgeon had come downstairs for some reason, and seen Jean. He immediately postponed his next operation, to save Jean's life. Surgeons with his kind of qualifications are hard to come by in Iran, and for him to be free at just that moment was, like so much else on that day, a miracle.

Was all this a series of coincidences? Or is there some other explanation why our lives were preserved that fateful May Day morning? Archbishop William Temple once said 'coincidences begin to happen when you pray.' Had there been people praying? Diana, virtually imprisoned with the children in that bathroom, not knowing what might happen, said she felt a strong sense of hundreds of people praying for us.

Perhaps this is the point to explain that we work for a missionary society (the Church Missionary Society, CMS) and that each of the missionaries wherever they are in the world are linked up with ten different churches in Britain. Christians in these churches take an active interest in their own 'link missionary' and try to pray for them and for the particular church they are working with. So that meant ten churches were praying for us. And we knew of others. One couple had written saying that they prayed for us twice each day, year in year out. That's a lot of praying! Since the early days of the revolution many had prayed for the safety of the church and of the missionaries working in Iran. Was it coincidence that things turned out as they did that morning?

Alone in the flat below, I had sat down to look out of the window. We often looked out in this way, seeing the chaotic traffic of the so-called one-way street beneath us, then looking higher to gaze out on the sprawling concrete jungle of Teheran. Further still the mighty range of the Alborz mountains rises majestically behind the city to the north, snowcapped even in early summer, untouched by the dirt and confusion of city life and seemingly untouched too by revolutions and counter-revolutions. In fact I stayed down deliberately that morning. I wanted to use the children's absence to 'lift up my eyes to the hills' and say my morning prayers. Was it perhaps just those prayers that were working to preserve the lives of Jean, my family and myself?

'Coincidences happen when you pray.' Maybe just as God uses our work to bring benefit to those around, so he uses our prayers to bring his love and protection to people we care for.

## Free to leave

Later on we became aware that this wasn't the only time our lives had been preserved. When we realized they wanted to kill us many advised us to leave as soon as possible. A member of the Iranian church came up to me the following Sunday evening after the service.

'Get out now,' he said, 'before it is too late.'

To get out of Iran we required an exit visa. There were administrative difficulties in getting this because it had to be issued in Isfahan where we had worked for five years before moving to Teheran. Each day's delay caused me some anxiety. We had a twenty-four-hour police guard, but we didn't know how long this would be provided.

I went several times with my Iranian colleague to the special building where they issued visas and permits. We spent hours trudging from floor to floor and from office to office. Nothing in Iran is simple – to the foreigner anyway! Each time we went I was told there was no news from Isfahan. In desperation we managed to get a contact with the colonel in charge of the whole visa-processing machine. He assured us the exit visa would be ready in a few days.

On our next visit we went straight to the colonel. In spite of all his previous promises he said I must now go to the Isfahan Revolutionary Court to get permission to leave the country. I knew that this court had made many difficulties for the Episcopal church, and that it was quite likely they would detain missionaries or church workers. This did not apply to Teheran which always seemed more lenient towards us.

What I didn't realize at that time was that if I had gone to Isfahan I would almost certainly have been imprisoned. This happened to Jean Waddell herself just ten weeks later, when she went to Isfahan to get her exit visa. Teheran had told her that they had nothing against her leaving.

I turned to leave the colonel's office. There seemed no other way. I must go to Isfahan. But at that very moment a telex arrived from Isfahan. I had already gone to another office in the same building. The phone went and I was summoned back to the colonel. He showed me the precious telex print-out.

'You are free to leave the country,' he said.

I left that building with a great sense of relief.

## Airborne

Less than a week later we were approaching the departure lounge at Teheran airport. We had gone through customs and all the other hurdles. Suddenly we saw ahead of us a small police kiosk. One of the two police officers produced a long list of names.

'Your name?' he asked.

This bewildered us. Slowly, so slowly, he began to go through the names. He repeated his question. Diana, holding the two children, turned away. The tension was unbearable. We were so close to leaving. Our lives were still intact. What if now we were prevented? My stomach felt empty and I felt a terrible weakness. Then he reached the end of the list and waved us on. We breathed again.

Airborne at last, Teheran was slipping away from us. I could see far below the monument built by the Shah in the early 1970s to celebrate 2,500 years of Persian monarchy. Now it was all broken up. A new Iran was emerging. This great region of the world could never be the same again. My eyes filled with tears as the city gave way to the desert. The words were still ringing in my ears which my colleague used as we took our leave of him that morning by the church door:

'Better to leave now and *ensha allah* (God willing) you have thirty more years to live, than to remain here and live for only three days.'

I knew he was right. In fact within ten weeks Jean Waddell was to be arrested, swiftly followed by the arrest and imprisonment of the three remaining pastors in the church, Dr John Coleman (with his wife, Audrey), Iraj Muttaheddeh and Nosrattullah Sharifian.

But though I knew in my head we were right to leave, my heart was not completely convinced. As I sat on that plane, part of me still lingered in Iran.

# 2

# BREAK-UP OF THE OLD ORDER

The extra-strong plate-glass display window at the entrance to the church compound next to our house in Isfahan had been shattered into a thousand pieces by a single bullet. This was in June 1978. Behind the broken fragments lay an open Bible – displayed in the window for many years. The picture of the Shah and his family was still there too. The window had been broken two or three times during that year. We put in the picture of the Shah believing that no one would dare break it again with his picture there. How wrong we were! The Shah's picture, so revered until now, was no longer a guarantee of anything. The old was breaking up. We gave up replacing the window and blocked it in with a piece of wood.

A few days later we heard that the Bible display window at the Christian hospital had been burnt. I ran up the road to see if this news was true. It was. The glass had been broken and the display section badly burnt. The beautiful Persian mosaic tiles on the wall were blackened by the fire. Amazingly, the Bible had not been destroyed. I even managed to take a photo of it as it lay open, surrounded by blackened debris. The old was fast breaking up.

In fact much more was happening beneath the surface than many of us were aware. The streets of Isfahan in the heat of that summer were filled with angry marchers. In Teheran the army was mobilized. Already strains were appearing in the armed forces. A young soldier shot his commanding officer and then shot himself. The students in the university were restless and militant. But the television was still strangely silent about it all. The Shah's figure still dominated the news. Press censorship masked the real situation.

## The fire burns

In mid-summer I went to Mashad in the north-east of Iran for a holiday. Diana had taken the children back to England for a month. It was obvious that the unrest had spread right across the country. The truth of the Persian proverb hit me forcibly: 'there is fire beneath the ashes'. The people were burning with anger and hatred against all the Shah's regime stood for. On the surface everything seemed more or less the same. The ashes were concealing the fire.

There was a twenty-four-hour bus journey through the empty desert. We ate rice and kebab and drank yogurt at 11 p.m. in a small-town restaurant. At dawn we stopped by a mosque and the driver ordered all of us to go and say our prayers (imagine that happening on a British coach!). I struck up an easy friendship with Ali sitting next to me on the bus. He taught me some Persian poetry (how they love it and remember it), and he even wrote some poetry of his own as we entered the sacred city of Mashad – burial place for over a thousand years of the much-revered eighth Imam.

But the fire was still alight. A university professor whom I met a few days later told me how fifteen students had killed two university servants who had interrupted their secret anti-Shah meeting. He also told me that when the Shah recently visited the city the only people to welcome him were thousands of schoolchildren who were taken to the streets in buses and given flags to wave. Six months before this would have been unheard of.

In the sacred shrine itself everything was as I had expected. Thronging masses dressed in black were surging into the holy courtyard. Every woman wore a *chador* (a veil to the ground which can be used to cover everything except the eyes). The sound of wailing and tears as they mourned the death of the holy Imam; the look of expectancy on the faces of those who hoped to receive healing – all echoed the intensity of traditional Islam. And in contrast came the ceaseless noise of cassette music playing Iranian and Western pop in the stalls and markets surrounding the shrine. I noticed that pictures of the Shah, usually everywhere to be seen, were conspicuously absent. The army kept discreetly at a distance. The people, an Iranian told me, had never forgotten that in 1935 the Shah's father had attacked this most sacred piece of soil. Nor had they forgotten that the Russians did the same in 1912.

## Exhausted

In August the Shah made a forty-five minute appearance on television. He tried his hardest to emphasize all that his government had done for the country. I remember him saying how many schools and hospitals had been built and how fatal it would be if Iran became 'Iranestan' – a satellite of the Soviet Union. He looked an exhausted man. I had never heard him speak so slowly. Then, first in Isfahan and soon after in all the major cities, martial law and the night curfew were imposed. At every crossroads in the city we were faced by tanks and soldiers. The leading army general in Isfahan spoke for nearly an hour on the penalties of breaking curfew. There would be no mercy – that person would be shot. His face was hard and unbending.

We had asked the Armenian bishop to supper on the first night of the curfew and we spent most of the evening discussing when it was to begin. There were conflicting reports. Was it 9 p.m. or 10 p.m.? I was reluctant to take him back to his home after the earlier time for fear of breaking the curfew. In fact we played safe and I was back just before 9 p.m.

One morning I walked up to the magnificent high statue of the Shah's father on a horse near the famous thirty-three arch bridge by the river. Tanks surrounded it. There were hundreds of village people shouting pro-Shah slogans through loud-hailers. They had been brought in from the villages and obviously paid by the government. Lorries and cars full of them hooted their way round the city shouting for the Shah. There was a radio announcement ordering every car to display a picture of the Shah on the windscreen. We had difficulty in finding one but eventually did. I saw soldiers forcibly remove a man from his car and take him away (where?).

Then there was the Abadan catastrophe. Hundreds were trapped inside a cinema and burnt alive. It was deliberate arson. Wild rumours circulated that the cinema had been showing an anti-Shah film. A government inquiry failed to get at the root of the matter. Culprits were found, but were they the real offenders? A few days later a new prime minister was appointed – the second change of government under the Shah within a few weeks.

## 'Keep moving'

I went, as often I did, into the beautiful 400-year-old theological college just off the main street of Isfahan. It was an ideal place to find some quiet and I absorbed the atmosphere of stillness. There was the clear, cool water where those who came to pray could wash themselves to be clean for their prayers. A stream running through the centre of the spacious courtyard watered the tall green trees and abundant grass. I would often sit opposite the delicately shaped pale-turquoise dome flanked by two minarets, gazing at the deep blue sky behind. In the heat of summer or the cold of winter the sky was nearly always the same colour. I sat there again. Suddenly my friend the doorman approached.

'Keep moving,' he said, 'you can't sit down here any more.'

Even in this quiet sanctuary there was unrest.

For weeks the Shah disappeared totally from the national media. Rumour had it that a member of his family had tried to kill him. Officially this was neither confirmed nor denied. I felt the country was leaderless – like a boat without a captain, drifting into deep water. Then his photo suddenly reappeared in the still-censored newspapers. There he was on his boat on vacation by the Caspian Sea; but it was obvious the photo was some years old. When we next saw him on the television he spoke and moved with great difficulty and pain.

The surprising thing was that although many Iranians thought the Shah could be overthrown, very few of the foreigners in Iran believed it could happen. He seemed so strong and secure. We simply failed to grasp that Iran was in a state of revolution. (In fact the word 'revolution' only began to be used when Khomeini entered the country.) It was the depth of the people's feeling that we so signally failed to understand. They equated the Shah with pro-West and anti-Islam policies. When their holy month of Muharram came round at the end of that summer, and religious feeling was running very high, the Shah was particularly vulnerable. I remember thinking that if only he could survive to the end of the month it might all die down.

Looking back now I can see that there was a deep unwillingness in me to face the break-up of everything I had known and loved in Iran. We had spent five years growing to appreciate and love the land and its people. Outwardly the country had prospered. Foreigners were welcomed; there was a sense of security and stability. The church was free to hold its worship and to share its faith in unobtrusive ways.

Inwardly I feared what might happen if all this was swept away. What would replace it? Where we saw the spectre of stability crashing about us, the Iranians saw the vision of a massive protest against corruption and secularized westernization. We were confused. It seemed that so much good had come through the Shah – prosperity; stability. Just a year or so before, President Carter had called Iran 'an island of stability'.

## Prophetic words

It was so difficult to see how God could be working in these huge, apparently destructive forces. I often recalled a conversation just a year before with Max Warren, the former general secretary of our missionary society.

'God is always surprising us,' he had said to me. 'You never know what he may be doing round the next corner.'

For me, facing this situation in Iran, those words were prophetic. Unwillingly, reluctantly, I and many others were being surprised by the sweep of events. Was this God's judgement on the excesses of our Western materialism and self-interest?

The vast majority in the world outside Iran were also caught out by what was happening. I read a few months later that the American Association for the Advancement of Science issued a survey to discover who in the US had understood what was happening in Iran. The survey found just one scholar who got it right. He was an Englishman who took an Islamic first name – a professor of history at the university of California. In 1972 he wrote an essay predicting that popular protests would continue and the appeals of such religious leaders as Khomeini would be widely heeded. No one listened to his voice. As always for every man with perceptive insight there were a hundred who couldn't see behind the status quo. It is a frightening thought when you consider that, in the US alone, there are a million people employed full-time trying to understand world problems and to guide government relations with other nations. A book called *Illusion of power* was published in the West in the early part of 1978. It was a brilliant account of the state of the economy under the Shah and of the evident corruption. But the author, for all his knowledge, came to the conclusion that an Iran without the Shah was impossible to contemplate. So few saw the fire beneath the ashes.

We were slowly beginning to realize that we were surrounded by millions of Iranians who saw their country through very different eyes from ours. They felt exploited by the extravagances of the regime – so obviously backed by Western interests.

An American friend of ours worked at the big new oil refinery in Isfahan.

'What would you do if we weren't here to make your refinery work?' he asked his Iranian colleague.

'Buy some more Americans,' was the caustic answer.

People began openly to question where all the wealth was going. Why was it that less than a tenth was reaching the industry of the country and the pockets of the people? Food prices rose alarmingly. The poor were particularly affected. Frequent price commissions were quoted in the press, but they didn't seem to do any good. Suddenly the electricity would be cut off and we were plunged into evenings of darkness. There wasn't enough power for domestic use because so much was being used by the newly-installed industrial plants.

## The Shah's picture

Meanwhile in other ways we saw the break-up taking place before our eyes. For two years I had been regularly visiting three young Iranian friends who worked in a copper-engraving shop. At lunchtime we would go to a nearby restaurant for a meal of *chellow kebab* (rice with meat cooked on an open grill), onions, egg, butter, and delicious, round, flat bread fresh from the baker's oven, with pepsi cola or a yogurt drink. Sometimes Ahmad, one of my friends, would ask his mother to cook a *khoresh* (stew), and we would sit on the floor in a small room off the shop.

The shop itself was simple. Everywhere lay huge copper trays on which they were hammering intricate Persian designs, copying the traditional patterns. A photo of Ali (cousin and son-in-law of Mohammad), wielding his sword, hung above the place where the *Ostod* (master) was working. As in every shop a picture of the Shah gazed down at us with benign confidence. That day when I went the picture had been turned round. I showed surprise at this. These young men had always resolutely defended the Shah. They said little in reply except that they were watching to see which way the tide would turn. The next week when I visited them the picture had disappeared altogether.

One of our Farsi teachers was a highly attractive young woman. Most of the missionaries rated her the best of the teachers – certainly she was the most expensive! She was always very fashionably dressed. A few weeks before we had sat on the richly carpeted floor of her home eating melons (Isfahan's special fruit), *shireenis* (sweet delicacies) and delicious lamb kebab which she had cooked herself. Suddenly she turned up in a black dress and black headscarf, and wearing no make-up. She told us she was fasting. We had never seen her like this before. She told us she could no longer be our Persian teacher. She must give herself totally to the revolution and fight for justice. She horrified us with stories of men the regime wanted to get rid of who had been dumped alive in the salt swamps and marshes to the south of Teheran and left to die. We didn't know how true these were.

## Death to the Shah!

Our daily life began to change radically. Suddenly petrol was hard to buy – in oil-rich Iran. Waves of strikes hit the oil fields. In earlier days strikes had been illegal (I'd never heard of one in five years). Now they were spreading right through the land. One morning I queued at 5.45 a.m. for petrol and arrived back for breakfast at eight. We only used the car when absolutely necessary. A picnic in the desert, something we always enjoyed, became a luxury because it meant using precious fuel. And anyway we wondered just how safe it was to go out of the city. An English friend of ours returning to England left his car outside our house; the few litres of petrol in the tank were more valuable to us than the car itself!

Every shop in Isfahan, except those selling food, put up its shutters and closed for four months. Imagine it! No buying of household goods, clothes or anything for four months. The streets seemed to be the setting for a great funeral. The huge bazaar was utterly silent. If any shopkeeper threatened to open he received harsh treatment from all the others. It was a total strike. And this was nationwide. The little food shop down the road fortunately remained open and so we could still buy our eggs, milk and vegetables. Three times a day (dawn, midday and dusk) the call to prayer rang out – louder and much longer than we had ever known it. As the days grew colder, paraffin for the heating stoves became scarce. This was the only form of heating. Only a tenth of the normal fuel was flowing up from the south.

The electricity cuts were now a nightly event. We would be ready and waiting, equipped with a collection of carefully hoarded candles. In the darkness we would sit and listen to the BBC world service news, in English and in Persian; this was our chief link with the outside world and only reliable source of information. One evening when we invited my

Jean Waddell, after her discharge from hospital. At this stage her ribs were still heavily strapped, which explains her rather portly appearance. She was imprisoned soon afterwards.

Iranian colleague and his wife for a meal, he brought his radio with him so as not to miss the news! For weeks and months no post arrived.

One lady was our most faithful Farsi teacher. She had begun to teach us on the third day after our arrival five years before. Now she began to arrive for our lessons wearing a black veil, which we had never seen her wear before. She arrived and left by different doors in the church compound to be sure she was not followed. She was afraid that her contact with Christians and foreigners had been noted.

At night the streets were strangely silent. No one dared to break the curfew. What, we wondered, was going on behind the high walls of the houses all around us? For my first few years in Iran I had hated those high walls. They seemed to cut us off from each other. But now I was glad of their security.

Then the fire began to break into flame. Regularly we heard marches and riots round the city. Gunfire was frequent. We wondered who was being shot. Sometimes at night we heard terrifying noises – loud sounds of shouting and gunfire. Were some people defying the curfew? Some time later we realized that it was mostly a tape-recording of the riots in Teheran, played through loud-speakers from the rooftops; just one more way of adding to the unrest. By day people marched down the street shouting 'Death to the Shah!' Walls were covered with anti-Shah slogans. Then the statue of the Shah's father was finally pulled down and burnt. Every other similar monument was toppled. Helicopters came perilously close to our roof-tops and dropped pro-Shah propaganda on to the streets. The headquarters of the secret police (SAVAK) was attacked and taken over.

## 'Keep the soil together'

In all this ferment how was our small episcopal church faring? Basically it consisted of a few hundred regular Iranian worshippers and some thousands of baptized people, in six different cities of Iran. Our bishop and five Iranian clergy were our leaders. How could such a small number, dwarfed by such vast revolutionary forces, make any worthwhile positive contribution? I remember the bishop saying more than once that if a seed is to be kept alive and have space and time to grow, the earth must be kept together. Soil erosion would lead to the death of the precious seed – in other words soil erosion was soul erosion. And so he saw the need for the church to do its part by helping in whatever way it could to build up its own life and the life of the nation – to keep the soil together.

This meant realizing the importance of 'people-hood': affirming all that was true and good in the nation of Iran. This could not be done if the church kept itself apart and distinct, but only as its people belonged to the nation as a whole. This is why, when he became a Christian, Bishop Dehqani-Tafti kept his Persian name, Hassan; he did not stop being a real Persian when he became a Christian. Jesus had spoken of Christians as 'the salt of the earth' – mixed right in with the food it flavours, yet needing to keep its distinctive taste if it was to do its job.

Yes, I could see that the church had to be part of the nation of Iran; to flow with the revolution; to feel some of the people's anger and frustration; to help build a new society. And yet it also had to be rightly distinctive. Just as Jesus himself was both fully a Jew, yet also the Saviour of the whole world who saw events from a much wider perspective than a narrowly national one.

It seemed a difficult but creative role for this tiny group to play.

# 3

# THE DESERT IS BEAUTIFUL

I never thought I would wake up on time for the mountain walk on that first morning. Five a.m. seemed so early, and to walk at that hour three times a week sheer madness! The bishop had already been doing this for five years. But after three months in Isfahan I joined him and one or two others on 'the walk'. For another five years this was to be a regular routine.

We would always leave 'on the dot'.

'Like your British trains,' said the Bishop, 'we always leave on time!'

My alarm clock only failed me once or twice in those five years. We would drive three miles south along the empty road. There before us was the huge, dark and, at that early hour, rather sinister shape of Kooh Sufeh (Sufeh mountain). Nothing else was visible in the darkness. The desert track, as we turned into it, was easy to lose, but somehow the bishop's car knew the mountain approach as well as he did, and we always managed to find the right spot to park.

First we walked up the long valley. We needed to go slowly, even the fittest of us. It was all too easy to run out of energy.

'*Yavosh . . . yavosh*' ('slowly . . . slowly'), we said to each other, '*nafas-e-ameeq bekesheed*' ('breathe deeply').

How fresh the air was after the pollution of Isfahan! It was a different world; far from the chaotic traffic and the screeching brakes of reckless drivers; far too from those high walls behind which we all lived. Here there was silence. Here there was space.

## Sunrise

After a steady half-hour of walking we reached what we called 'the first stone'. We would pause and feel the texture of the rough stone with our hands. In that half-light of early morning it was a familiar friend. We never passed it without stopping. As we looked back down the valley, rays of light, the first of the sunrise, appeared over the distant mountains.

Ten minutes more and we reached 'the second stone'. This had a flat top and was much bigger. Gradually a tradition grew. Any newcomer on the walk, and there were many, including the visitors, were asked to climb to the top of this rock. Together we stood facing the rising sun. In English or in Persian we said the words from a verse of the Psalms:

'From the rising of the sun to its setting,
The Lord's name be praised.'

At just this time the sun would begin to appear. There it was, a great ball of fire hanging in the middle of the emerging cloudless blue sky.

Then we climbed a short, steep escarpment. Occasionally we would turn left and come upon a ridge immediately below the top of the mountain. This view was breathtaking. We were facing away from Isfahan. The early mist hung in the valley beneath us. It was like a great empty basin with desert, more desert, and still more desert, leading on to another range of mountains. Beyond, there was more desert and yet more mountains in the hazy distance. We could see no sign of civilization. The next city was hundreds of miles away.

But usually we turned right, towards Isfahan. We loved to run down some of the gentle slopes and experience the feeling of freedom. Then we stopped to gaze at the city beneath.

Some say it is set like a jewel in a ring of mountains. We could see the whole of the city surrounded by desert, and then the distant snow-capped mountain peaks beyond. The Zayandeh ('life-giving') river wound its way through the sprawling city. Then it lost itself in the vast salty wastes of wilderness.

Where the river went there was green in the desert. Away from it, all was barren. To me it was a constant symbol of my own heart. To leave the living water that Christ gives me is to become dry and empty. Stay by it, and there is abundant life.

Sometimes, looking back from the lower slopes of the mountain, we could see its top caught by the rays of the rising sun. For a few moments its red glow changed the bare rock into something like fire. And then it was past, and it looked ordinary again. Rapidly the sun became brighter – too bright to look at, even at such an early hour. It lit up the dome of the Shah mosque, away in the heart of Isfahan.

'It gives a feeling of security,' said the bishop, 'to see that mosque.'

I knew what he meant. Whether from that spot on the mountain, or flying in by plane, or standing on the roof of our flat, it was our great familiar landmark. I never tired of looking at its beauty.

As we drove back through the congested city, joining the rush-hour traffic, we passed groups of men standing at the crossroads in the streets, holding shovels and pickaxes. They were waiting for their day's work – hoping someone would come and hire them. Employment was a very uncertain thing.

The traffic jam on the bridge often held us up. Hooters were never used sparingly! But somehow we felt different people. We'd seen such beauty – the rising sun, the azure-blue sky, the vastness of the desert, the distant snow-capped peaks. It was a good way to start the day.

Rudyard Kipling said you only begin to know a country when you start smelling it. For me the smell of the fresh mountain air, the slow walk up that long valley, the exhilaration of running down those slopes – these made me feel that I did belong to the land and to the people, for all I was a foreigner. I was 'at home'.

## Barbed wire

One time, when the three of us all happened to be clergymen, we found ourselves comparing the walk to a church service. Whether you follow the prayer book or the Catholic mass or a free type of service, each has its own structure and form. You get attached to it. It may even become part of you with prolonged use. And within its structure you begin to find a freedom. Through those words you know so well (the Lord's Prayer for instance), you often find a new meaning shining out; or that hymn you've always sung can come alive in a new way. 'The walk' was like this. We knew it well. Going to the mountain three times a week for five years makes 750 times! Whether we went in the thick snow of winter, or in the spring with the wild flowers growing out of the hard soil, or in the dry heat of summer – always we received something fresh and lovely from Kooh Sufeh.

'The Spirit of Jesus is like the early morning breeze,' wrote the Persian poet.

I knew a little what he meant.

One day our car slipped over the side of the desert track and down a slope as we tried to reverse and park in the darkness. I went to find help, leaving the bishop to guard the car. Astonishingly, ten men appeared from nowhere! They joined together and began to heave it up towards the level surface.

'Ali, Ali,' they chanted in unison, using the name of Mohammed's son-in-law.

It seemed a strange way to rescue the bishop's car! We knew then that we were never without friends on the mountain.

As the Shah's control over the country was threatened, the army took control of the mountain. They were going to use it for military exercises. Posts were erected. We wondered what was happening. Barbed wire followed. Finally signs were put up bearing a skull and crossbones. *Marg* ('death') was written on each one, threatening death to anyone who went beyond them.

We came there one morning, just as these signs had appeared. We were about to begin the walk up the long valley. We really didn't believe those signs were directed against us. We felt the walk had as much right to go on as the mountain itself had to exist! As we drew closer we saw a uniformed man pacing up and down. He was an army officer, deliberately placed there to warn us and other mountain walkers.

'You can't come here any more,' he said stiffly.

He wouldn't answer any of our questions. He had his orders. It was a hard blow. 'Our' beloved mountain was closed. This filled us with foreboding. If they could do this to the mountain, what else might they do? Our walks continued (they had to!). We went along the river bank instead, but our hearts were still on Kooh Sufeh.

With the overthrow of the Shah and the collapse of the army, the mountain was opened up again. Those horrible signs of death disappeared, along with the barbed wire. We were overjoyed. But slowly we began to fear. The church was increasingly under pressure. The bishop's life was in danger. Friends warned us not to go on the mountain unless there were at least three of us.

'If I am killed, I am killed,' said Bishop Dehqani, several times on the walk. This was no fatalism. It was the courage of a man able to look death in the face, with all its uncertainty and fear, and to know that beyond it was the certainty of resurrection.

After we had moved to Teheran I went back to Isfahan for

one night on what turned out to be my last visit. I got up early and drove the bishop's land rover on that familiar route to the mountain. I was alone. The bishop was away. But without him it wasn't the same. He and the mountain belonged together.

## Make a desert

At other times, usually in early or late summer, when the weather was less hot, we went on a walk in the desert – 'the long walk' we called it. Nosrattullah, one of the Iranian clergy, would often join us.

Leaving early we drove out into the desert, looking back at Kooh Sufeh. One of us carried the breakfast in a rucksack. We walked for one and a half hours, passing between huge rocks which had remains of ancient fortresses on top of them. These had been built by the *Assassins* a thousand years ago, when they fought against the ruling powers. We made a detour round a nuclear plant the French were building – even here we could not escape man's pollution.

Then we arrived at Joozdon, a village the Afghans had destroyed in an attack 250 years ago. Only the pigeon towers remained. These were still used by farmers who collected the valuable pigeon manure and used it for growing the famous Isfahani melons. We sat under the shade of one of these towers and ate boiled eggs, the round flat bread, cheese and cucumber, and drank tea.

Somehow this taste of desert life had a deep but almost unconscious effect on my life. The great, empty spaces made spaces in me too.

'Make a desert in your life,' wrote Carlo Caretto, a Roman Catholic priest who himself went to live in a desert to find God.

By those words he didn't mean that we must all be like him and go to live in a desert. He meant that we need empty spaces inside us so that there can be room for God in our lives. I know for myself how easy it is to be so active and busy that I have no space for God.

One way we tried to make this kind of space was to use a little room in our home in Isfahan as a place of quiet (we were lucky to have one for this purpose). We put in it just a chair, a small table with a cross and open Bible on it, and a picture. Diana and I tried to go in there sometimes for a few minutes to 'make a desert'.

A young man called David came through Isfahan on his way to India. He worked in a Burtons clothes shop in London, but, like so many others, he was fed up with the rat race of our acquisitive society. He gave up his job and his security and left for India. He told us he was searching for God, for 'something real', as he put it. On Christmas Day he came to church. One of our friends gave him a Bible. He stayed for a few days and began to read it. He found what he was looking for. Later he wrote from India and told us that he had gone to Persepolis, the ancient capital of Iran, and there among its magnificent ruins, on New Year's Eve, he 'offered his life as a living sacrifice to God' – his words. Two years later he wrote again. He was back in England, studying at a Bible college, hoping to go back to India and teach the Bible there.

## Everyone prays

We visited a small village near Yazd, the big city in the middle of Iran's desert plateau. We had some friends in Isfahan who knew people in this village. They told us we must visit them. Would we really be welcomed? We'd never met them. They could only have heard of us vaguely. We waited for the bus.

'When will it come?' we asked a little impatiently, as a man gave us the tickets.

'*Allon, allon*' ('now, now'), he said.

We knew that could easily mean another hour, but in fact it came within half that time. We were surrounded by a magnificent, rugged range of mountains on the journey.

When we arrived at the village two small boys immediately wanted to be our guides. First they showed us where to buy nuts and sweets in the bazaar. No guest ever goes empty-handed. Then they took us to the house we were looking for.

Our fears quickly evaporated. Majeed and his family made us feel at home immediately. We all sat in the main room. It had no furniture, but the carpet was beautiful, and we sat on the floor eating fruit, leaning against rather gaudy cushions. Then Majeed's wife served us with rice and meat. Hussein, a friend of theirs, came and took us to his orchard. He told us to take as many peaches as we wanted. Then we returned to our hosts and they showed us into the same room so that we could rest. We hadn't realized they assumed we needed to rest. To our utter astonishment mattresses were put on the floor and they locked the door behind them, taking the key to ensure we would not be disturbed! Fortunately they came back and let us out two hours later.

When they wanted us to stay the night, we explained that we couldn't (secretly fearing a further spell of confinement).

'Will you come again?' they kept on saying, 'our doors are always open to you' – a phrase often used in Persian. We knew they meant it.

In a taxi on our way back to Yazd we met two Iranians who worked in the copper mines. They were very friendly and asked a lot about my work. When they got out to leave they insisted on paying our fare. The hospitality we received that day seemed unending.

The following day we visited the home of Homoyoon, one of the last Christians left in Yazd. She had become a Christian through the work of the Christian hospital, destroyed in a fire many years ago. Her house was very simple and clean. It had two rooms and there was a well outside in the middle of the garden. She welcomed us so warmly. Her father was very old and not too well. He lay on a mattress on the floor and quoted Persian poetry nearly the whole time we were there! Another Christian friend joined us and Homoyoon asked me to take a service of holy communion. It was the first time I had ever taken it using the Persian language, Farsi. It was an unforgettable experience.

Within eighteen months Homoyoon had died. Someone said it was as if a light had gone out in Yazd.

I was struck by a sentence in a book I read before going to Iran:

'The vast deserts of Iran lead people to believe in the reality of God quite naturally.'

The people, the writer claimed, are deeply religious. For them there is no separation of spiritual and secular – everything is governed by God. We knew the Persian phrase well 'everything is in the hands of God' – it was used in everyday speech all the time.

When we visited a village near to the town of Natanz (eighty miles north-east of Isfahan), we felt very much this deep religious feeling. We picnicked by a stream in the shade of the trees. A group of children, as so often, came to watch us. One of them, an older boy, plucked up courage and came towards us.

We asked him his name.

'Ali Zadeh,' he said.

He offered to show us the village.

'4,000 people live here, but only 500 stay in the winter; the rest go to Teheran to find work,' he told us.

I was amazed that the population moved so easily between this village and the city.

'Everyone prays here,' he said, as he showed us some of

the thirteen mosques in the village.

I wondered if this was true.

In the oldest mosque a woman, her face withered and weather-beaten, lit a lamp and showed us a precious piece of equipment – a generator providing electric lights for the mosque when they were needed. To our astonishment we discovered that this was the only electricity in the village. The mosque, with its lighting, was obviously the focal point of the village. Apparently a mullah came from Teheran twice a year, in the month of fasting and in the holy month, to lead the prayers.

Ali Zadeh then led us to his house.

'*Befarmoyeed*' ('welcome'), he said, using the most common of all Persian words.

We explained that we were short of time and couldn't accept his welcome.

I looked at a sign above his front door:

God: Mohammed: Ali

Fatimeh: Hassan: Hussein.

This was the holy family of the prophet. But God's name came first. It was this deep religious feeling in the ordinary village people that struck me so forcibly.

## Love the land

'Learn to love the land as well as the people,' Bishop John Taylor told us as we first left for Iran. He was at that time leader of our missionary society.

The church owned a house in a village called Soh (seventy miles north of Isfahan). It was here that we really learned to appreciate the beauty of the land and to love it.

The house itself was one of the few brick ones in the village. The others were made of mud and straw. Downstairs, opening out on a little courtyard, was a small dark room where one of the girls of the family was weaving a carpet. It took her six to nine months to complete it. In the courtyard was a well with a leather bucket from which we drew our water. The ceilings of the upstairs rooms were made of sticks, cleverly woven together.

I remember a morning walk. There was a herd of goats and sheep with bells round their necks, making a beautiful timeless sound as they drank water from a stream. A donkey (a villager's most valuable possession) snorted as he came round the corner carrying a huge load of maize and wheat, twice his own size! The soil itself had many different colours – yellow, brown, red – all blending harmoniously together. A dried-up river eddy was a reminder that in winter, after the snow had melted, water would flow again (*ensha allah*, 'God willing'). How much they depended on the melting snow. A little lizard darted in front of me, in hot pursuit of a blue beetle. I saw three wild dogs in the distance chasing a hare; the desert was full of these dogs. A man stood alone in his field, erect and motionless, his hands stretched out before him, facing Mecca. He was saying his midday prayers.

As I returned to the village the owner of a small orchard offered me grapes and apples. He told me he had known Dr Wild when, twelve years before, he had gone to the Christian Hospital in Isfahan for medical treatment. In the village again, with its mud walls, I saw the dispensary open for vaccinations. A woman was making her own bread over a stick fire in a dip in the ground. Smoke came out of the chimneys of the bath-house – there were separate times for the men and the women. An old man was squatting on the ground; he counted his beads, ninety-nine of them, each representing one of the beautiful names of God. A little man sat in his shoe shop, working away with his hands. Everything was unhurried. Time itself seemed to stand still.

That evening I went to the mosque. I took off my shoes, as is the custom, and sat at the back. A mullah was chanting the

Qur'an and saying his prayers. No one else was there, but it didn't seem to matter. To him the important thing was worship.

As the day wore on we sat on the flat roof of our house. Slowly the sun slipped over the barren mountains, sending shafts of light into the gathering darkness. At 8.30 p.m. we were plunged into darkness as the electricity went off. We slept deeply, refreshed by so much that was lovely.

The following day we had a donkey ride. Jane, my sister, and her friend were with us. The old man who was in charge of the donkeys gave one of them to each of us to mount. I wondered if I could survive for even five minutes, as my donkey had very much a mind of its own! He was the one who decided where to go! All I could do was hang on. The old man had a secret 'donkey language' he used – weird noises came from his mouth – he must have wondered why we laughed so much, but the donkeys seemed to know what he was saying as they would change course or speed according to the noises he made. We rode for an hour through a fertile valley, close to a stream. We stopped for lunch. How our legs ached! Again we were invited to help ourselves to pomegranates from an orchard.

On the way back I got off my donkey to take some photos. Then came the problem. The donkey wouldn't stop. I couldn't get on again. He kept running and I clung on to his neck. The others were laughing too much to be able to help, but Jane valiantly dismounted and heaved me on. I sat again in triumph, feeling for once that the donkey hadn't got the better of me. But when I dismounted again to take another photo (or was it to give my legs a rest?), the donkey broke into a trot and with great confidence entered the village on his own and went to exactly the right house, where he waited for us. I think he was glad to be free of this foreigner who only knew how to drive a car.

### Perspective

What was it that attracted us to these village people? That welcome we received at Majeed's house; the simplicity of Homoyoon, with her deep faith; Ali Zadeh's willingness to show us his village; the beauty of Soh – they seemed to have a quality of life which I longed to possess. 'Contentment' is the word that sums it up. They didn't seem to be always wanting to get things. There was satisfaction in their daily living. They weren't continually fighting against the clock. They had time to 'sit and stare'.

This was a real challenge to our set of values.

'Getting and spending we lay waste our powers,' the poet said.

After a week in another village I wrote down various suggestions for our lives:

'If we don't need it, don't buy it.'

'Don't mind what other people think.'

'Be content with what we have.'

This was a badly needed perspective.

# 4
# FOREIGN INVASION

I found myself sitting precariously on the back of a motorcycle on a warm afternoon in the late summer of 1978. A young Iranian had stopped and offered me a lift. He went at great speed and I held on for dear life. Traffic regulations in Iran seemed very few. 'If there is a space, fill it' seems to be the national motto for motorists! We did just manage to stop at some red lights. Two men, obviously Westerners, passed in front of us. My driver turned back to me and shouted above the din of his engine:

'Every American should be killed.'

I wondered if he thought I was an American too!

A few minutes later I dismounted. As we shook hands I told him that we foreigners had been invited to his country by the government. He disappeared into the distance, to fill the next empty space. I knew for certain that we were far from welcome.

We had landed at Isfahan airport in the middle of January five years before. As we flew high above the clouds on the forty-minute journey from Teheran we could see the rolling tracts of desert, and then the mountain ranges covered with snow, like a beautiful pure white cloak. What a total contrast as we came down the steps of the plane! Around us in their hundreds were US helicopters. We had heard vaguely of the build-up of American military equipment but it meant nothing to me until I actually saw this massive array of aircraft.

On our first Friday when we went to the English-speaking service in the church we met some of the pilots and other employees of Bell Helicopter. Other Americans were working for the aerospace programme, and yet others had come to Isfahan to build a large new textile factory – the biggest yet in Iran. Within a year there were ten thousand Americans in Isfahan and several times that number in Iran as a whole. British firms began to arrive too, but they were mainly based in the desert in a purpose-built town thirty kilometres out of Isfahan. The Russians were not to be left out, though we saw little of them. They lived near the large steel works they had built outside the city. We saw their buses coming into Isfahan on Fridays (the official rest day), but we had the impression they weren't allowed to talk to anyone and must stay in their own groups. Only one ever came to see the church. It became increasingly obvious that the Shah wanted to make Isfahan the largest industrial and military complex in Iran.

## Pepsi Cola Street

Soon we saw other towns rising in the desert to accommodate the newcomers. Schools with American teaching programmes were started. Churches multiplied. A big new oil refinery was planned. Pizza and hamburger shops sprouted everywhere. Foreign clubs opened. In casual conversation you heard new names for some of the streets – Mehr Street became Pepsi Cola Street because it was near to the Pepsi Cola factory.

Many lived Texan-style in Iran. Shopping was in big supermarkets where prices were high. Many lived for weeks or months in the big new hotels before they found accommodation. A localized peanut butter famine was alleviated by a special consignment flown in from the States by one particular firm. Rents quadrupled rapidly. Iranian landlords preferred letting their houses to foreigners because they paid more and were not there too long. The Iranians couldn't compete in this sort of market.

Yet it was a difficult situation for many of the foreigners. Some wives would never go out shopping because it meant using Farsi in the local shops. Also you had to use local taxis which involved standing in the road shouting your destination to every passing car – which might or might not be a taxi. Others didn't know their address because they couldn't pronounce the street name. Ignorance of the language set a big gulf between them and the local people. In this atmosphere misunderstandings abounded.

On the other hand many Iranians were attracted to a Western style of living. One of our friends was an English

A desert scene near the village of Soh, about seventy miles north of Isfahan, where the Anglican church in Iran owns a house.

architect. He had the task of designing one of the new towns. He loved the Persian style of building; the small courtyard with its pool and fountain, and leading from it the different rooms with their round arches over the doors. It gave a feeling of togetherness; each part related to the whole through the common courtyard. He wanted to build the town on this model, with narrow streets so that community feeling could be fostered. But he was sadly disillusioned. His Iranian employers told him that he must design buildings in Western style. The apartments must be separate, built upwards not sideways, and the roads must be wide.

The helicopters, the high rise apartments, a whole Western lifestyle – it all seemed to signify a kind of foreign infiltration into the country. In its 2,500 years of monarchy Iran had known many invasions; the Greeks, the Arabs, the Turks, the Mongols – the list goes on. Iranians know what it is like to live with foreigners banging on their door. Was it this kind of feeling that got to that young Iranian on the motorbike and made him want to kill the Americans?

## Imperialists

Certainly I didn't see myself or the foreign community in this way. But then my blood was not Persian; nor did Iran's history of invasions run in my veins. A Persian wrote this in the official English-language newspaper after the Shah had left:

> 'For over 2,500 years we have been ruled by imperial regimes which opposed our people, but only a few of them caused irreparable destruction; they include the Arabs, the Mongols, the British which was the blackest of all and which forced on us the Pahlavi dynasty of the Shahs, later enforced by the US. The destruction caused by these rulers has never been fully repaired and we still suffer greatly from these past serious injuries. Thanks to

the imperialists, the users, none of our past grievances was ever heard and none of the criminals responsible for them has ever been tried or questioned.'

Certainly how we see ourselves is very different from how others see us.

If I didn't see myself as an invader I did sometimes become very conscious of being an intruder. A few months after our arrival we joined the members of the English-speaking church on a day's outing to the Soh village, about 110 kilometres north of Isfahan. The church owned a house there. For fifty years missionaries had gone to this beautiful secluded village in the middle of the desert, for holiday and relaxation. Now there were sixty of us going in a large bus. We travelled on the main Teheran road for nearly an hour, then turned off on a desert track towards the east. The bus stopped at a large caravanserai, built in the sixteenth century as a rest place for travellers on their donkeys and camels. Its high walls enclosed a spacious courtyard which now was filled with sheep. I wondered how we seemed to those simple shepherds with cameras, transistors, flashy clothes. It must have felt a bit like an invasion.

We arrived at the village. It was typical of hundreds. The houses were all made of mud. There were no tarmac roads and no street lamps. The electricity was only turned on for a few hours each evening and that for only some of the houses. There were no glass-fronted shops and for most of the homes the only water supply was from the well. Secondary schools were unknown. Our bus made a strange contrast to the donkeys and to the women carrying water containers on their heads.

Our worship service was held in the garden of the church house. We didn't want to draw undue attention to ourselves and cause difficulties. Our Bible reading was the story of the Samaritan woman who met Jesus as she came to the well and was offered the water of eternal life. Just then a village woman quite unselfconsciously walked past us and went to the garden well to draw her water. For me at that moment the world of Jesus and the world of Soh seemed so close together. And yet to the village people, as they gazed at us from a distance, following Jesus was now associated with wealth, power and, by their standards, rather scanty clothing. Our prosperity divided us from their world.

## Shekoofeh

Shekoofeh came to work in our house one day each week. She was in her early forties but looked fifteen or twenty years older. She had worked from childhood. In fact while weaving carpets as a child she had lost the sight of one eye through an infection (her donkey couldn't get her to the doctor in time). Her sister had died and she supported their three children. The husband had left many years before.

She had a lovely smile and rarely complained. Once she had a vivid vision of Jesus, and in all her difficulties she found strength in her faith. We often wondered what she thought of our Western-style house. We weren't getting a big salary – in fact our allowance was just sufficient to keep us – but how did we appear to her?

We soon knew the answer when we visited her home. We realized we must seem like millionaires. She came with us in the car to show us the way. We went through many narrow lanes and were glad no car came in the opposite direction! Then came a walk through a long narrow passage of mud walls leading to a courtyard. At the side was a well with a bucket for her and the neighbours. A beautiful old Persian arch flanked her doorway.

Shekoofeh's house was one room. It was very tidy and swept. The walls were plastered but without paint. Half the floor was covered by a cheap cotton rug – a present of which she is very proud. There were no chairs; she sat on her roll of bedding. The only other items of furniture were two little tables; on one was a gas ring (no oven) and a kettle, and on the other two saucepans and a few plastic dishes, spoons and forks. There were two little Persian-style alcoves in the walls, and in one was a small pile of clothes which we realized was her total wardrobe. Three old pairs of shoes were in the disused fireplace. There was an electric light attached to the wall. On either side of the door through which we entered was a window (there were only two) and a shelf. One shelf had a few cups and saucers and a teapot, the other had two old tins containing her total pantry. That was all she possessed.

We began to realize what was missing. Water. That was drawn from the well in the courtyard – washing facilities and toilet she would have to share elsewhere. Cooking equipment (apart from those two saucepans), extra bedding, anything decorative, anything for entertainment, cupboards and drawers; all these were missing. We could see everything she possessed. She didn't need a cupboard – she had nothing to put in it!

We drank coffee which she had bought in specially for us (tea was her drink), and ate bananas (another luxury). I thought of all the gadgets we had – the fridge and the freezer to name but two. How alien our lifestyle must seem to someone like Shekoofeh.

## The iron skeleton

Our church life was naturally affected by the presence of 10,000 Americans in Isfahan. The effect was symbolized by the two congregations, English-speaking and Farsi-speaking. Every Friday morning the church was filled by well-dressed Americans and Europeans who mostly came by car (causing rather a jam!). There was a sense of activity and organization. Many were thrilled to find a church and came regularly.

The Farsi-speaking congregation was half the size. Only two or three came by car. Their material standards were much simpler. It took much courage for many of them to come to church because they were from a Muslim background. Their concern was less with numbers and more with just keeping their Christian faith alive in a difficult and sometimes hostile environment.

It was through a joint building project that the two congregations came face-to-face with each other and experienced their great differences. The English-speaking congregation had money to spare and wanted to extend the church buildings. The Iranian Christians were glad of the proposed improvements to their church but yet deeply resented the way it seemed to be imposed on them. For a year there were many meetings and hours of discussion but no agreement proved possible. Then came the revolution and the plan was dropped.

On a bigger scale the same thing happened in Teheran. A large church was designed and the English-speaking congregation promised to provide most of the money. Reluctantly the Iranian Church agreed to the project. The work began with great vigour. I stayed for a week in the nearby guestrooms and every night suffered the deafening noise of bulldozers working under the arc lamps. The foundations were established. Huge iron girders were erected. Then some of the foreigners left. The money ran out. The revolution came. And the Iranian Church was lumbered with a vast, ugly skeleton. In retrospect it is easy to see that the project was wrong-headed and far too ambitious. This was not the kind of building the Iranian church really wanted. They would have been far happier with something much smaller. When we moved to Teheran and lived for seven months next to that iron skeleton, I was reminded how we foreigners had tried to impose our standards on the church. It was a subtle form of invasion.

## Drink, sex and violence

One devastating misconception became evident the longer we lived in Iran. Ninety-eight per cent of Iranians are Muslims. It is a Muslim country. They think of the West as Christian in the same way that they see themselves as Muslim. And so they assumed that all we Westerners were practising Christians. Only those Iranians who had visited the West or were better educated knew how false this was. With Western prosperity came the inevitable drink, drugs and other problems. The films they imported were stuffed with sex and violence. So naturally they looked at the behaviour of all the foreigners and assumed that this was 'Christian'. What a frightening misunderstanding!

The feeling of being at the mercy of the Western powers was not new to the 1970s. All through the nineteenth century Britain and Russia were constant rivals in Iran, which felt itself to be a pawn in a large power struggle. Britain needed a neutral Iran to safeguard the road through to India. Russia always feared their southern neighbour becoming a tool of the West. In a sense the discovery of oil in 1908 made the country even more dependent on the foreigner, because Britain controlled the main assets. In the understated words of a historian: 'Feelings of resentment and humiliation were engendered in the Persian people.'

What this did to the Iranian national soul is well expressed by the Persian poet Bamdod:

I am bothered by a pain - which isn't mine.
I have lived in a land - which isn't mine.
I have lived with a name - which isn't mine.
I have wept from grief - which isn't mine.
I was born out of joy - which isn't mine.
I died of a death - which isn't mine.

On 16 January 1979 the Shah left Iran. He was never to return. He took with him some precious soil from his Iranian homeland. Perhaps it symbolized his deep, lifelong identification with Iran. The next day I talked with an Iranian friend I had known for a few years. He told me, very honestly, that he looked on the foreigners as thieves who had broken into someone else's house and stripped it almost bare. I didn't try to argue with him. I knew – perhaps he did too – the good that we had brought to Iran. But it all faded into insignificance beside his deep feeling of being exploited and misused. The longer I stayed in Iran the more vividly aware I became that we had much to answer for.

# 5
# THE WALLS ARE HIGH

I sat in my study on a cold afternoon on 19 February 1979. The room was separated from our house by an old Persian courtyard, which was surrounded by a mud wall with beautifully shaped arches. There were two wells for drawing water, though one of them had been blocked up. I was trying to prepare a sermon for the following Friday church service.

Suddenly my peace was shattered. Rupert, an English surgeon from the Christian hospital nearby, burst into the study and threw himself on the other chair. He was in a state of shock. I had never seen his face so white. I knew there was bad news. With great difficulty he told me that Arastoo Sayyah had been murdered. Arastoo was the Iranian pastor in Shiraz (about 600 kilometres south of Isfahan). He told me

I was wanted for a meeting in the bishop's house immediately.

I went straightaway. Some of the church staff had already gathered. Two or three wept silently. All looked dazed and numb. We only had five Iranian pastors. We knew each of them well; it was a close-knit team. Arastoo was the senior pastor. It seemed utterly unbelievable that this had happened.

## Murder

The bishop shared all he knew about the events surrounding the murder. Like any minister Arastoo had his friends and his enemies. His study was in a secluded place some way from the house. Two young men had come earlier that morning asking to see him. One of his sons took them to his father. When Arastoo didn't turn up for lunch they went to find him. He was lying on the ground with his throat cut.

I remembered Arastoo well. I had met him in London when we first knew we were coming to work in Iran. He had encouraged us and been very kind. Like most Iranians his manners were impeccable and he showed great respect to everyone. He delighted to tell me how, when Muslims came to inquire about the Christian faith, he would lead them to a place where they could see the roof of the church. It was built with a mosque-like dome, but on top of it was a cross. He would point up to that cross and explain the meaning of the sacrifice of Jesus. Of all the pastors he seemed to be the one who could lead others most naturally to share his own deep faith.

At that meeting the bishop put into words the question which was in all our minds.

'Was this an isolated incident or were we all to meet the same end as Arastoo?'

There was no answer. We could only guess. We wondered

how members of the church would react to this devastating news.

'This is either the end or the beginning of the church,' the bishop said.

A few days later the pastors met for their prearranged annual meeting. At the holy communion the bishop read from the book of Revelation. Tears filled his eyes, and ours:

'These are they who have come out of the great tribulation; they have washed their robes and made them white in the blood of the lamb . . .'

The wine, symbol of the poured-out blood of Christ, seemed to have an added meaning as we drank it at that small gathering.

We met afterwards to talk together. Suddenly the prepared agenda didn't seem important any more. Instead – death and how we would face our own when it came.

'If I am killed, I am killed,' the bishop said.

I felt the colossal strength of his dedication to the will of God.

We had a long discussion on the use of church buildings for worship. One of the pastors felt we should abandon them and meet in different homes. This way he felt the church would keep a low profile and not draw attention to itself. I spoke, at the bishop's invitation, and said I felt the church buildings were important for worship. In the church we were linked with the past and this gave a sense of continuity and strength to Christians. I felt that our courage and sense of identity would be stronger if we met in church buildings for worship. The majority agreed. The churches remained as the focus of our weekly services, although we knew that this risked the safety of pastors and people alike. This same issue was to come up again fifteen months later when only three pastors were left in the church. Again they took the same courageous decision.

## The martyr's voice

Two weeks later the church in Isfahan was filled with people for Arastoo's memorial service.

'Martyrdom is a gift of God,' said the bishop in his sermon.

He quoted some words of T. S. Eliot about God using martyrdom to speak to the cruelty of men. As I thought about these words it came to me in a fresh way that maybe this is the only way God really can speak to cruel men intent on murder. Arastoo knew he was in danger. He had been warned by his church committee to move his study away from that secluded place into his own house. For some reason, although he agreed with them, he had delayed. When he visited us in Isfahan a few weeks before, he seemed to sense that his life was far from safe. Yet he chose to remain with his people. Only the power of the love of God shown through such a man was stronger than man's hatred.

'If they will not hear the voice of the martyr, they will hear no one,' said the bishop in that same sermon. 'When the corn of wheat dies it springs into new life. The important thing is that we all remain faithful, whatever the cost . . .'

Those high walls around us were filled with a new meaning. Originally they were built round all the Iranian houses to protect the women from the gaze of men. But I saw now that they also served to feed the fear of men and to keep the unwelcome intruder away. There had been too many invasions, too much insecurity, for anyone to feel safe in Iran. The high walls might make us feel a little safer, but they also made men more suspicious of each other. We wished they had been high enough to save Arastoo.

In the last years of the Shah it was commonly said that in every group of three people one was an informer of SAVAK, the dreaded secret police. No wonder trust was difficult. In the words of a Persian proverb 'most men have a hundred faces'. Therefore never trust the face you see. It meant no one spoke freely, even to close friends.

## Exodus

The days before and after the murder of Arastoo were filled with uncertainty for the foreign community. The Shah had left the country on 16 January. All the car drivers in Isfahan hooted their horns with delight as the news spread. This was something they always did at a wedding. For the first time for many months people were smiling again. It seemed the whole country was rejoicing, although many were anxious about the outcome. We then wondered for days when Khomeini would arrive. Rumours abounded. The Shah's last prime minister, Shappor Bakhtiar, tried against increasing odds to keep his government together.

Meanwhile foreigners were leaving the country in their tens of thousands. Law and order seemed to have broken down. We knew the prisons had been opened, and there had been a virtual free-for-all in the armouries of Teheran. The loyalty of the army was under increasing pressure. We saw pictures in the papers of soldiers accepting flowers from the crowds and putting them in their guns. No wonder there was an exodus.

Three weeks before the Shah left, our church had been filled twice over with 300 people, mostly foreigners, for a performance of *The Messiah.* By early March virtually every one of them had left and our English-speaking service was closed. I wondered if any other church had emptied quite as fast! Feelings against the foreigners were now more openly expressed. Slogans such as 'Yankee, go home' and 'Death to the imperialists' were written all over the walls on every available space. Everyday life for us continued as before but obviously the situation was very unstable. Although so many of our British and American friends had left, Diana and I did not feel the effect too greatly. All along we had felt that our real roots were with the Iranian church. It was from them that we gained our strength and support at this time.

With the political situation in the country so uncertain a group of us met each night for half an hour or more to pray in the chapel of the Christian hospital. One such evening I got a vivid sense of two contrasting but equally real dimensions. Walking over to the hospital I'd seen pillars of smoke and smelt the fires in the city. The whole sky was alight, as cinemas, hotels, banks, any buildings associated with foreigners, were burnt to the ground. That was real! And here we were praying together, believing in a God who could overcome our fears; in what the apostle Paul called 'the peace that passes all understanding' (a phrase he wrote from a prison cell). That was real too! In fact the reality of God seemed more true now than ever before. Either God really did exist and was just as real as anything else, or he didn't exist at all. There was nothing in between.

I was a member of the British Security Committee, representing the twenty-five or so missionaries working with the church. We met regularly to assess the deteriorating situation. The committee shrank weekly as more of us left the country. In the end only three or four were left. We were told that there were four stages in the plans for evacuation. Stage four represented the final evacuation of all foreigners. And we had very nearly reached it.

Preparations for such an evacuation were well under way. The Americans were to be responsible for airlifting the whole of what was left of the foreign community. The British had already evacuated all foreigners from Khoozestan province in the south-west. It was seen as quite a possibility that the widespread riots could lead to the whole of Isfahan going up in flames. Such was the total breakdown of law and order. A re-grouping area was named and a map of the one exit-route from the city given to each member of the security committee. All civilian airports were closed so we would use the military one. We were told to have our petrol tanks full (if that was possible with the shortage) and to be on the alert for immediate departure. Those we represented had to be informed of these plans.

Then a cable reached us from the British Ambassador in Teheran:

> 'The situation is now very unpredictable. Living conditions are likely to become more difficult. Our ability to render assistance may become very limited. We can arrange aircraft for those wishing to depart as soon as the airport opens and will let you have details. Meanwhile I urge you:
>
> a. To make all necessary preparations for an early departure if that is your intention.
>
> b. To let us know your intention.'

Diana and I agonized over what to do. We had an eighteen-month-old baby to consider; and Diana was five months pregnant. Our families in England were naturally extremely worried. Some were putting great pressure on us to return immediately. Yet we felt identified with the local Christians. To leave them now would be to discourage them at their most vulnerable time. We found ourselves torn in two. Should we stay and risk whatever might happen? Or should we give in to the many pressures and return? The bishop, when he talked with us all, hoped the missionaries would stay but said that anyone was free to leave if they felt they should.

Our own missionary society had always stressed that it was the local Christians who should decide what the missionary should do in an emergency situation. But they also said that a missionary should feel free to leave if he or she felt it advisable. Danger itself, though, was not sufficient grounds for leaving.

We both knew it was right for me to stay. We were seen by Iranian Christians as part of their church. If I left it would be desertion in their eyes. Our uncertainty was whether Diana should leave with our child. If she went, we knew we were likely to be separated for the rest of her pregnancy and for the birth – possibly longer. There seemed no clear way forward. For foreigners like us, just as for local Christians and other religious minority groups, like the Jews, there was a great fear of the unknown.

We spent a sleepless night trying to work out what was right. Then the next morning we talked with Margaret, the bishop's wife. We knew she would understand our position, but would also speak out of her own experience of Iran. She told us of a similar situation nearly thirty years before when the country had supported an earlier prime minister who had opposed the Shah. The Shah had left the country. The missionaries felt very precarious in their position, but those able to stay, who were not deported, felt that in staying they had made the right decision. She suggested that we stayed for forty-eight hours to see if the country did erupt in flames when Khomeini returned. So we waited. And somehow the situation seemed to get better rather than worse.

From that moment we felt it was confirmed that God wanted us to stay. Diana read out some words of the apostle Paul:

'And we know that in all things God works for the good of those who love him, who have been called according to his purpose.'

We knew that God was in control; that he had a purpose in what was happening, and in allowing us to be there. It seemed now we were living in a different dimension altogether. There was much fear and uncertainty. It seemed the walls had never been higher. Yet, if God was God, somehow he must be working for good even here, even now.

## Khomeini arrives

It was at this time that a final cable came from the British ambassador in Teheran. He told us that the last British plane was to leave Iran in two or three days. After that the Embassy could no longer be responsible for those who had chosen to stay.

Rumours and counter-rumours filled the air for some days. The country was waiting breathlessly for the Ayatollah to return after his fifteen years of exile. One moment we were told he was on his way from France. The next moment this was denied. Finally he arrived. On the television we saw the overwhelming, tumultuous welcome he received. The aged hero, seen by many as God's messenger to his people, had come. For them he was in the true sense the Ayatollah, the 'Sign of God'. Crowds surged round him as he came off the steps of the plane. He disappeared altogether from view. Then his car was unable to move forward because of the crowds. The thronging masses waved from roofs, trees, every conceivable space where they might catch a glimpse of him. 'Freedom' was the word on everyone's lips. The days of repression were over at last. They felt a new age had arrived.

As the television programme ended we were astounded to see the familiar smiling picture of the Shah for a few fleeting seconds and to hear the tune of the national anthem. Someone still seemed to support him, and had the courage to show it. Was this a sign of the real situation? Perhaps not everyone was so wholeheartedly supporting the Ayatollah after all. But that picture was never seen again.

A few days after the murder of Arastoo, my colleague Iraj and I decided that we must burn the English-speaking congregation's hymn books. Each one had the printed title 'Armed Forces hymn book', and at this point we were destroying everything that could be construed as pro-Shah material. It was one of the most difficult things I had to do in the revolution. The hymn books symbolized so many people who had used them in our worship and who had found a living faith in Christ for themselves. Their friendship had enriched my life so much.

As we threw the books into the flames I thought of Rosemary, a young American mother, who one day told me she had *run* to church to worship, so thirsty was she for the presence of Christ and of other Christians. And there was Ernie, a helicopter pilot, who with his wife and son had found a new faith while living in Isfahan. There was Garry whose hobby was wrestling; he'd taken me to meet his Iranian friends in the wrestling stadium and had talked to them about how much Jesus Christ meant to him. And how could I ever forget Sharon who had played so many of these hymns on the organ? 'Amazing Grace'; 'The Lord's my Shepherd'; 'The old rugged cross'; my mind was ringing with them. As the flames licked up the pages, Iraj led me back into the church. He led us in a prayer. I had no words. But I knew we'd done the right thing to burn the books. The memories of the people would never go. And it was people who really mattered.

Our daily life continued. But it was very much living from day to day, not knowing what might happen. On our early morning mountain walks the bishop quite often expressed his willingness to be taken or even killed if that was God's calling for him. He bore a tremendous burden as leader of the church. One day on the mountain a man shouted to me in Farsi. I couldn't quite hear him. I thought he said I would die if I continued with the mountain walks. In fact he had said I would undoubtedly succeed if I kept them up. It showed just how much fear I had built up inside me.

## Take-over

One day in May an Iranian friend came to see me. For five years we had known each other. Others had told me not to trust him. I didn't completely, and yet I valued his friendship. I said goodbye to him as he left our door, and watched him as he went out of the big, blue, iron church gate. Something inside me told me to follow him. There on the other side of the road he was talking with a young man whom I knew was an informer against the church. I felt bitterly disappointed. No wonder it was said of Jesus: 'He did not trust himself to anyone because he himself knew what was in man.'

That same young informer came to see me a few days later. Seven others were with him. They stood by the door inside the church grounds waiting for me to come. I felt their attitude was hard and aggressive. They said they wanted to talk to me about Christianity. I told them I would willingly talk with one of them but not with all of them at once. They became very hostile. They wanted to talk with Iraj. I went to see him and he replied in the same way. I held my ground. At last they realized I wasn't going to change. They left and said they would be back. I felt that a great power of evil had been at work in them. I was glad I had the necessary strength to be firm.

One month later, on 11 June 1979, the Christian hospital was taken over. For several months members of the local Revolutionary Council, a powerful group put in charge of the main affairs of the city when Khomeini took over, had stationed themselves in the hospital, allegedly to make a report on the hospital's activities. In fact, looking back later, the missionaries and other Christians working in the hospital realized that these men were slowly drawing the Iranian staff over to their side and inciting rebellion.

And then the take-over came. I got a phone call that June morning which sent me racing over to Ron Pont's study (Ron was the Medical Superintendent). He was talking on the phone, trying to find out from different people in the hospital

A group of clergy with the bishop after John Coleman's ordination in autumn 1979 (John is second from the left). The man with the moustache is Nosrattullah Sharifian, pastor at Kerman, who preached at the service. In the cassock is Iraj Muttahedeh, pastor in Isfahan. John, Nosrattullah and Iraj were all later imprisoned.

what the situation was. Over a hundred of the hospital workers were shouting for him to appear. They had drawn up a list of demands, one of which was that British missionaries should leave. It was true the main positions in the hospital had always been filled by British missionaries as there was great difficulty recruiting Iranian Christian staff. This was obviously no longer acceptable. We felt that if Dr Pont went to meet the workers he might even be killed. But if he stayed they might equally well come to fetch him. A nasty dilemma. Dr Rupert Fawdry acted as mediator between the mob and Ron Pont. How we prayed for God's guidance at that moment. Then he saw clearly that he must not go.

Dr Pont never entered the hospital again. Within a few weeks he and the other British missionaries who had been working in the hospital left the country. The take-over had astounded us all. It seemed an ironic twist of the revolution that those who had done so much for the hospital should be treated in this way.

The next day the bishop, who was in Teheran, sent us all these words which had been a help to him that very morning in his own devotions. An Indian Christian, lying in hospital waiting for death, had written this for a friend:

'God leads us along such unexpected paths.
Look how I have been led,
Tossed hither and thither for the last year,
And now the unknown.
We are leaves in the wind,
Specks of dust,
Flakes of foam.
Only let us be faithful,
And with great love and obedience
Allow ourselves to be wafted where God's
Will is guiding us.'

## A new life

Diana was just over eight months pregnant and it had been planned for her to go into the Christian hospital for the delivery. Now where was she going to have the baby? We decided on our house. Medical equipment was smuggled out of the hospital by friends, and Diana's doctor, Rupert Fawdry, stayed on for the birth. On the day all went as planned with the help of her doctor, an Iranian Christian midwife and one of the British missionaries who was a midwifery tutor. We nicknamed baby Deborah 'the little ray of sunshine'. She was so gloriously unaware of all the darkness and fear.

Fortunately there was always another side to life as well. By this time alcoholic drink was banned. The phone rang and Diana answered it. A member of the church said: 'Tell Paul I'm going to deliver ... er ... something.'

She realized he thought he was being overheard. He asked her to go immediately to the church door and open it to let his car in. By now Diana guessed what was happening and did as he asked. A car moved in and two men got out. They looked round carefully to make sure no one was around. Then in total silence they took a large cardboard box out of the car and carried it into the back entrance of the house. Still without speaking they got back into the car and drove out through the church gate. Diana locked it behind them. In the house she opened the box and then called through to me:

'Paul, we've some more wine for holy communion at last.'

# 6

# MUSLIMS OUR FRIENDS

It was a strange dream Diana had soon after our arrival in Isfahan. She saw a mosque jumping over the wall and coming towards us.

I tried to work out its meaning in the days that followed. Somehow the mosque down the road seemed such a different world from the church compound where we lived. Three times a day we heard the call to prayer from the top of the minaret relayed through a loud speaker, in these twentieth-century times, and often through a tape recorder! It seemed a far cry from the church bells which, in a much gentler way, called Christians to Sunday worship. How could that mosque jump the wall?

Maybe it was the loud speaker which seemed to emphasize the difference. There was the mosque, supremely confident in its message:

'There is no God but Allah and Mohammed is his prophet.'

At any hour you went there, someone would be praying or quietly chanting the Qur'an to himself. At midday prayers on Friday it was filled to overflowing. 'God is God,' the call to prayer seemed to be saying, 'he is all-powerful; he alone is God; leave your work and come and worship him; nothing is important compared to him; *allah-o-akbar* – God is greater; beside him there is no other.'

In comparison the peal of the church bells on a Sunday evening seemed rather gentler. No less they beckoned the faithful to worship the one supreme God, but the faithful were very few compared to the mosque. They too were saying that God is great, he alone is to be worshipped. But enter St Luke's and your eyes are drawn to the cross standing on a polished table at the far end of the church. 'God is great. Come to him through the death and resurrection of Jesus.'

Could there be a meeting of these two worlds? Would the mosque really jump over the wall? But perhaps the mosque saw no need to do so. Was it we as Christians who must go towards the mosque?

## The cabinet-maker

Early on we were able to meet some from the world of the mosque. We needed to buy a kitchen cabinet. A shop in the main street displayed the kind we wanted so we went in. We were met by Parveez. We always called him by this name as his second, family name seemed so difficult to pronounce. We bargained for a price – this is the way of doing things in Iran.

Later, when he came and put it up (by hammering two nine-inch nails straight into the wall!) he invited me to go to the mosque the following Friday. This certainly seemed the reverse of Diana's dream! I gladly accepted, though I felt a little fearful as the time grew nearer. I began to understand a little how people who are not Christians must feel before they enter a church for the first time.

I left my shoes at the door of the mosque as everyone else did. This was a holy place. Those who were going to pray washed themselves as a cleansing ritual by the pool of water. I entered the prayer hall, equivalent to the main part of a church.

I sat crosslegged at the back with my head slightly bowed. I was apart from the others and felt rather cut off and out of place. No other foreigner was there. In front of me were rows of men, bowing to the ground, then kneeling and touching the ground with their foreheads. They did this in perfect rhythm with each other; none was out of time. One very old mullah with a full-length beard came and sat near me. Another mullah led the prayers from the front, chanting the Qur'an.

'*Allah-o-akbar*' – 'God is greater' rose from the lips of all the prostrating men.

Parveez arrived late and came and sat in front of me. His young son dutifully followed his father's every action. Yet another mullah, responsible for the sermon, climbed up a small staircase and sat on the top. He gathered his brown robe around him and began to speak. The hush was full of expectancy. I wished people listened like this in church! After fifty minutes he was still going strong, and he never once referred to any notes.

I was greatly surprised when little glasses of tea with lumps of sugar were passed round halfway through the sermon. I felt I might be left out, but I wasn't.

In fact, that day they were celebrating the death of Mohammed's son-in-law, Ali. I gathered that the sermon was based on all that happened on that fateful day in the seventh century when Ali was murdered while praying in a mosque. As he reached the climax of the sermon, tears poured down the face of many of those around me. Some beat their foreheads with their hands. They seemed to be sharing the very sufferings of Ali himself. The women, invisible to us on the other side of a curtain, joined in the loud wailing. I asked myself when last I had wept for the sufferings of Christ. I don't think I had ever shown my grief like this. Then the sermon ended. Everyone stood and held their hands silently in front of them. It seemed to symbolize a kind of emptiness in their lives which God alone could fill. Then they turned to each other and clasped hands. The sense of brotherhood, of belonging to each other, seemed very real.

Parveez immediately came and invited me to supper. He sent his older son in the car to fetch Diana. We felt a bit apprehensive as our knowledge of Farsi at that time was so limited, but we needn't have feared. They made us very welcome. We sat on the carpet eating fruit and rice and meat. His wife was expecting their ninth child so we saw nothing of her, although we were aware of all her activities in the kitchen. The daughters served us with food. They wore veils over their faces all the time. We looked with admiration at Persian carpets hanging on the walls. Parveez explained that each one had taken two years to make in the bazaar. He told us that he was a *hajji* – one who had made the sacred pilgrimage to Mecca. We understood that he was a much-respected man in the mosque.

He told us of the great admiration he had for Dr Schafter from the Christian hospital who, over twenty years before, had operated on him successfully. Two years after our first meeting, when Parveez was ill and had chosen to go to the Christian hospital, he sent a message asking me to visit him. It seemed a strange thing that a Christian minister should be summoned to the bedside of a Muslim *hajji*.

## A few fanatics

For three months I regularly attended the mosque each Friday evening for prayers. Finally, after the prayers had ended, I was invited to attend a class for those translating the Qur'an into other languages. They told me it was being held in a garden somewhere in Isfahan. Parveez told me there was nothing to fear and encouraged me to go. I accepted the invitation rather reluctantly, not knowing why I had been asked. About thirty people were there, all men, and all drinking tea and eating melons. We sat in a circle and talked with each other. After an hour three men approached me.

One of them was a mullah and one introduced himself as a professor of French at the university.

'What have you learnt about Islam after coming to the mosque these three months?' they asked.

I tried to explain as best I could (I had only been learning Farsi for three months). I said how much I admired the way Muslims prayed three times a day.

'Why do you come to our mosque?'

I explained that we Westerners were very ignorant of Islam; that we must learn more about it; that in a sense all of us, Muslims and Christians, were searching to know God more deeply. I added that we would welcome to our church any who wanted to come and find out about the Christian faith.

Suddenly the men began to get really angry.

'If you want to worship in our mosque you must become a Muslim,' they said.

I repeated that I only wanted to learn more about Islam. This only increased their anger.

'I don't want to cause offence,' I said. 'I am a guest in your country.'

The professor shook his fist at me. I really thought they might attack me.

'You must never come to our mosque again,' they all said.

Their voices were threatening and they were shaking with anger.

I felt shattered and defenceless. The atmosphere had changed so suddenly. I was alone in face of an anger I couldn't really fathom. Somehow I felt rejected by the very people I wanted to understand. I was glad to get away and find my way home. I knew my aim was right, but obviously my presence in the mosque had been a threat to some of them.

A few days later I met Parveez and told him what had happened. He was obviously very unhappy.

'Most of us in the mosque welcome you,' he said. 'It's just a few of the more fanatical people don't want you to come.'

His continued friendship meant a great deal to me. I knew that I mustn't judge Islam only by its fanatical elements. There were those who wanted bridges to be built between the very different worlds of our beliefs.

In the days that followed I often thought of that university professor shaking his fist at me. I hoped that one day we might meet again and find a way to be friends. Then a few months later our family were having supper in a restaurant. (Like all Iranians we were learning to eat out in restaurants much more. The food was good and inexpensive.) I suddenly saw the professor at the far end of the restaurant, sitting at the head table of what looked like a wedding celebration. I wondered what I should do. It would have been easier to have ignored him, but I felt it was an important moment. So I took a deep breath, went over to his table, and introduced myself. He held out his hands, I took them and we clasped hands for fully half a minute. He even invited me to his house.

## Friendship - and . . .

In the years that followed I got to know Parveez fairly well. Often I would sit in his cabinet shop. His son would fetch us tea and nuts, and would recount for me some story in the Qur'an. Obviously he had a very deep concern that I should learn all I could about his religion. One day Diana found us each telling our own versions of stories about Abraham – his from the Qur'an and mine from the Bible.

Strangely he hardly ever asked about our faith. As he saw it, he was the teacher and we were the ones to learn from him. But perhaps he had listened more than I realized because, on Diana's birthday, he came to our house and gave her a cross to wear round her neck.

Another time Parveez arranged a meeting in his home for us to meet some of his Muslim friends and talk with them about our beliefs. We accepted the invitation but were a bit unsure what the outcome would be – like people setting sail in unpredictable weather conditions. They were anxious to show us how wrong we were to believe in Christianity.

Each time they would ask us: 'How can you say that Jesus Christ is Son of God? How can God ever be involved with the material world? God is Spirit. He alone is the One God. He is far above us. He could never become a man and live in this world, as you believe.'

We tried repeatedly to say that we too believed that God was One. He had no rivals. He was supremely powerful. He was Lord and Creator of all.

'But what if God should *choose* to show his power by becoming a man? What if he *chooses,* out of love for us, to get mixed up with this material world? Mustn't we admit he has the freedom to use his power as he chooses?'

Time and again in these conversations we experienced how quickly we could become frightened of each other. This could make both sides more aggressive and less inclined to listen to what the other was trying to say.

They wanted to go on meeting, preferably every evening. But we felt the discussion was becoming more like an argument. There was no openness. It brought back to my mind what a long-term missionary, Norman Sharp, had said to us when we first arrived in Iran:

'You can never win a Muslim by argument. Show him the beauty of Jesus.'

The meetings ended, but we were glad to find that our friendship with Parveez and his family continued.

## The coppersmith

About a year later I met Reza. I had very much wanted to

meet a younger Muslim friend, and one day I prayed specifically that I would meet one. That same day I wandered into a copper-engraving shop and watched a young man hammering away at a copper tray. I admired his artistry – the way the finely-cut pattern of flowers was slowly emerging. We chatted and he offered me tea. Then he invited me to visit him whenever I wanted.

I adopted the habit of regularly calling on Reza and his two young friends – all working under the steady eye of the shop-owner. Sometimes Reza would leave abruptly and return twenty minutes later. He had gone to say his prayers; nothing would stop him doing that. Often we went to a local restaurant and the four of us would eat chicken and rice and drink pepsi colas; Reza or I would pay the bill. He was small in height and lame in one foot. His parents had been divorced when he was six months old and his grandparents had brought him up. Marriage was an urgent priority and he asked me to look around for a suitable wife for him!

One day he came to us for tea. I was interested to see how much more aggressive he was about his faith when on our territory. He became the true missionary, urging me to become a Muslim. Whereas back on his own ground in the shop, he was always far more open. Plainly if real contact was to be made it had to be the Christian who moved towards the Muslim.

Another time he and his two friends had lunch with us. I wondered what they would think of our attempts to eat Irani-style, sitting on the floor – with Diana cooking rice and stew. Later Reza told me that the thing that struck him most was how we gave thanks to God before the meal.

Another day, when we were walking down the road together after lunch in our restaurant, he took my hand in his. I knew this was an Iranian custom, which meant he accepted me as his friend. When I told Diana about it she got decidedly cross. She and I never held hands in the streets of Isfahan! It was usual for the husband to walk a little ahead of his wife and physical contact was just never seen. Once, when we were walking together through deep snow, Diana slipped. Iranian men were walking past in pairs – hand in hand and comfortably upright. I did take her hand then!

Quite often Reza would question me about my own faith.

'Why don't you fast like we do?' he asked one day, in the heat of summer.

It was Ramadan, and each day for that month of fasting he and all true Muslims ate and drank nothing from sunrise (4 a.m.) until sunset. This was in temperatures of over ninety-five degrees fahrenheit. I tried to explain that in the time of Lent some Christians did fast because Jesus himself had fasted forty days in the wilderness. With shame I thought of how my resolution had failed the previous Lent. And anyway, what was that compared to his total fast? He had such a deep commitment to it. This was his way of holding more firmly to his belief and of fighting off the power of evil.

The following Lent I vowed to fast, but only from after breakfast until supper. Inwardly I felt quite proud of myself. At the end he asked me how it had gone.

'But did you drink anything?' he said.

I answered that I had drunk tea and coffee as I considered this was all right.

'Oh no,' he replied. 'Your fast has no value at all if you drink. You were not committed enough.'

When we were due to move to Teheran he came to say goodbye. Like Parveez before him, he brought a little cross for Rosemary, whose birthday was near.

'I hope you soon become a Muslim,' he said.

Somehow his gift and his words didn't match.

'*Be omeed a khoda* (in the hope of God) we will meet again.'

## The young mullah

I always remember the afternoon Diana and I went browsing in the large covered bazaar. It was the most exciting place in Isfahan. There were thousands of different stalls, wonderful smells of Eastern spices, never-ending piles of Persian carpets, ceaseless bargaining on every side, and much pushing and jostling everywhere. We paused at the door of a mosque right in the middle of the bazaar. A young mullah came out of the door, gave me a friendly smile and seemed willing to talk. His name was Ali and he was a theological student studying to become a mullah. What was my job? Where was our church? He was happy to accept a Gospel of St Luke in Farsi, and invited me to visit him at his college later that week. Then he gathered his robes round him and soon disappeared into the distance. Although a small man, he looked very impressive with his beard, white turban and flowing brown robe.

I was delighted to have this opening, and a few days later I was banging at the door of his college. The doorman showed me up a steep flight of stairs on to a flat roof. In his room which led off the roof, Ali was saying his prayers. I silently slipped off my shoes, sat cross-legged and watched him. I was glad he felt free to continue his prayers even with his guest sitting at such close quarters. Somehow I felt he had his priorities right.

His room was very simple and bare. Bedding was rolled up in one corner, and there was one shelf with books on it.

His prayers over, he shook my hand warmly. He made some tea on a gas ring and started asking lots of questions. Did I believe in God? Who then was Jesus Christ? Did I pray?

He told me he had read the Gospel I'd given him and had found the names of Elizabeth, Mary, Abraham and Moses – all of whom he knew from the Qur'an.

Other questions quickly followed. What was my salary? What was my daily programme? Then he asked if he could come on holiday with us the following week.

I couldn't imagine any of our English friends asking this! But Ali really did feel he had a right to join us. Why should it matter that we'd only just met him?

On subsequent visits I felt deep down that he was a lonely person. Somehow he lacked Reza's conviction about his faith. He certainly never tried to make me a Muslim. I felt he was hungering for something freer.

Then he came to visit us. Interestingly, he left college wearing his brown robe and white turban, but took these off in the car and arrived in his ordinary clothes. We assumed that he didn't want to be recognized visiting us. On subsequent visits he became bolder and came in his official dress. He wanted to see the church and I showed him round. How did we pray? Did we kneel or stand or sit? I showed him our Persian prayer book and also the hymns we sang. He was fascinated by it all and amazed that we had Iranian priests and Iranian Christians. He hadn't even known the church existed.

One day he invited me to join him at the evening prayers in the Shah mosque – the most impressive of the many fine mosques in Isfahan. I'd often seen the great door closed at dusk to all except those who came to pray. Others, like myself, were turned away. Now I was to have the opportunity to enter the inner prayer hall with my robed friend. I followed him in. Ali sat in front of me and the prayers began. As so often in a mosque I prayed silently to Christ.

The doorman approached. He asked Ali who I was. There was animated whispering. Then Ali asked me to leave with him. He was rather embarrassed and ashamed because of the situation he'd put me in. As a foreigner, I was not permitted to be there. (This was some time before the revolution with its anti-foreign feelings.) I said I understood and told him not to feel embarrassed at all.

'It was a privilege to have been there even for twenty minutes,' I said.

Ironically enough, it was Christians who were to cause the end of this friendship. As the revolution gained in strength it became more and more difficult to know who to trust. The doors of our church compound were now continually locked, and we kept a very sharp watch on who came and went. Some residents of the church compound were very concerned that only people whom everyone trusted should be encouraged to visit. It was felt we should ask Ali not to come any more. I still went to see him occasionally. But somehow the barriers were going up again. Open friendship was becoming difficult.

## 'Reality . . . reality'

There were other friendships. For some years I had heard about a particular sect of Islam called Sufism. The Sufis were those who emphasized the deeply spiritual part of their faith. They stressed the belief of the heart. For them to love God and be drawn ever closer to him was the essence of Islam. All over Iran there were Sufi prayer houses.

One day a friend of mine from Sri Lanka met a young Iranian on a bus journey. He was wearing a special badge and my friend asked him about it. He explained that he was a Sufi and invited my friend to visit his prayer house. He went the next day, met the Master himself, the much-revered spiritual leader, and asked this 'holy man' if he could bring his English friend.

This was how I found myself sitting opposite the Master on a cushion on a carpet, eating fruit and drinking tea. About ten of us sat in the room for three hours. I knew it would be disrespectful to change the position of my feet, but the experience was well worth my increasing cramp. For quite a lot of the time we sat in silence. When other friends of the Master entered they bowed deeply and kissed his hand. The Sufi Master was obviously held in tremendous awe. The man next to me whispered that I must never disagree with the Master.

'The Master,' he said, 'will know in his heart if you are opposing what he is saying.'

Those around me hung on every word the Master uttered as if it were the very word of God himself.

The Master's eyes twinkled at his own wit and poetry. He was saying deep things about God.

'God can only be known by love, not by thought,' he said.

He talked about the meaning of inner silence through which alone we could be united to God's love in our deeper selves. I took out my notebook to write some things down.

'There you are,' he said. 'You Westerners are all the same. You have to think everything out and write it down. Your faith is not rooted in the heart.'

Hurriedly I put the paper and pencil away! Then a cloth was set before us and deliciously cooked rice and kebab brought in. We were to be his guests for lunch too. At least now I could change the position of my aching legs!

As I got up to leave I asked if I could return another time.

'This is a house of God,' he said. 'Your Jesus is ours too; he was the greatest Sufi of all. You are always welcome.'

I did as the others had done, kissed his hand and backed towards the door so that I did not turn my back on him.

For the next eighteen months I went regularly twice a month to the time of prayer. First I would sit shoeless in the hallway. Others would be sitting there with me in silent prayer. Tea would be served in the small glasses. No words were spoken but each person was acknowledged as he came in. Then after half an hour we went into the prayer hall. A notice, almost untranslatable into English, was written in

Farsi over the door. A friend there told me only a real Sufi could understand its meaning. It said something like:

'Silence – the present moment is worth everything.'

It was something I needed to learn. The past I too often regretted. The future I too much feared. The important thing was learning to live in the present moment.

This friend was called Hussein. He was a man about my age, with a magnificent Persian moustache. Always he wanted to chat away and practise his English on me. He gave me books on Sufism so that I could learn more about it. He had a great reverence for Christ. One day he asked me why the disciples forsook Christ at his moment of greatest need on the cross. Then he turned to me and asked:

'Have you ever forsaken Christ?'

It gave me an uncomfortable feeling. He, a Muslim, seemed to be bringing me, a Christian, back to the roots of my faith.

## Seekers for God

Inside the door there was an octagonal prayer room. A large photo of the Sufi Master hung opposite the door. Each person who entered bowed in humility and touched, with the right hand, his forehead, his heart and finally the ground. The room was beautifully carpeted with cushions placed evenly round the walls. But otherwise it was totally empty. God alone, they believed, could fill the emptiness.

An elderly bearded mullah, called the sheikh, sat with head bowed to the ground. Since the Sufi Master was usually resident elsewhere it was the sheikh who was responsible for everything in the prayer house. I sat on a cushion with my back to the wall. About twenty-five of us were gathered. I was the only foreigner, but I felt they accepted me.

Again there was silence. No one raised his head. We needed to be very humble before God. Then one of the group took up a volume of the poetry and lyrics written by the Master. He began to sing them in a deep, rich voice. Every few minutes the others joined in with the words '*Haq . . . Haq*' – their word for 'reality'. They were searching for God, the ultimate reality. A young man next to me began to weep. His hands were stretched out before him. He longed for the reality of God. In the silence, the chanting and the tears I felt a deep sense of openness to God. Another glass of tea was handed round with sweets too this time. It was the humility of the place I loved. All were seekers for God. No one could have enough of him. And they allowed me to be part of their quest.

In the summer of 1979, as the revolution gained in intensity, I continued to join my Sufi friends. One evening, as we sat in the prayer room, the sheikh called for Hussein and whispered to him. Hussein beckoned me to join him outside.

'I don't know how to say it,' he said. 'I feel very embarrassed but the sheikh has asked that you do not come again.'

I asked him why.

'Others will think we are connected with foreign spies if they see you coming here,' he replied. 'We have nothing against you, but we are frightened about what may happen.'

It was hard for me to say goodbye to Hussein and those Sufi seekers. They had opened up another world of Islam for me – a gentler, less ruthless world. They believed that God could be found through the way of love and tears and prayer, and above all through silence.

'We can never say that another man is unclean,' said Hussein. 'We are all part of that same substance created by God, part of humankind. God loves each of us.'

In stumbling words I tried to say just how much his friendship and the experience of the prayer house had meant to me.

'Remember,' he said, 'that behind all our silence there is the struggle to find God.'

He kissed me, in Iranian custom, on both cheeks. He seemed to feel the parting as much as I did. As I walked along the narrow lanes to the main road and then home, I could still hear in my ears the chanting of the Sufis: '*Haq* . . . *Haq:* Reality . . . Reality'.

# 7
# THE PRICE OF FREEDOM

I sat drinking tea in the house of a young friend, Rahim. It was early January 1979. The Shah was still in Iran but everyone was wondering how much longer he could stay. The whole country had turned against him. Only the army was still loyal, and even that loyalty seemed uncertain. Rahim's eyes were lit up in a way I hadn't seen before. He had just returned from evening prayer in the mosque. The mullah in his sermon had told them all to be willing to give their lives for the revolution.

'We must die for our freedom,' my young companion said.

He took up his Qur'an and kissed it, as all Muslims do before they open it. Rapidly he turned to the passage he wanted and read it to me in the Arabic. In the English version, printed next to the Arabic, it read:

'And what though ye be slain or die when unto Allah ye are gathered . . . Allah giveth life and causeth death, and Allah is seer of what you do.'

In the coppersmith's shop. Reza has broken off from beating out the pattern on his tray to talk to Paul Hunt.

His sense of commitment seemed so complete.

I realized how Rahim represented the vast majority of people who took to the streets, facing the tanks and guns of the strongest army in the Middle East. Justice, freedom and truth were their deepest desires, and they looked to the revolution to bring them.

There was a poster stuck to every wall and shop window:

'Martyrdom is the heart of history.'

Another one showed the bodies of many killed by the army. Beneath it were the words:

'With all their hearts they went towards the bullets.'

## Arise and soar

Khomeini's words, on tapes and broadsheets, circulated everywhere.

'The Friday prayers are the means of mobilizing the people, of inspiring them to battle. The man who goes to war from the mosque is afraid of only one thing – God. Dying, poverty, homelessness mean nothing to him. An army of men like this is a victorious army.'

*Shahadat* (martyrdom), this was the heart of history.

'If you kill you are victorious,' said Khomeini, 'if you are killed you go to heaven.'

Was it really surprising that the TV screens were filled with what seemed mass hysteria? Since the days of Mossadeq, thirty years before, no one had felt free to shout these words in the streets. The people had lived under rigorous press censorship. Criticism of the Shah or of his regime had been impossible. Those who tried it were either killed, imprisoned, or, like Khomeini himself, exiled. Now, at the moment when it seemed the Shah must fall, the army and secret police were powerless against the united will of the people.

The opportunity to experience the meaning of justice,

freedom and truth had been denied them. Yet, like the rest of humanity, this was their search. They really thought that now it could happen.

I began to realize how much we in the West take for granted the freedom we have. I remembered the story of an Iranian who went in his car to Hyde Park Corner in London. He was astounded to hear people denouncing God and the government, making inflammatory speeches against everybody and everything. Then he saw a policeman approach.

'Ah,' he thought, 'now he's come to arrest them all.'

But the policeman came up to him:

'Would you please switch your engine off, sir. We can't hear what the speakers are saying!'

We need to value our freedom far more than we do.

The words of the Persian poet Hafez, written on his tombstone in his home-town of Shiraz, were now filled with new meaning:

'Where are the tidings of union? That I may arise.
Forth from the dust I will rise up to welcome thee.
My soul like a homing bird, yearning for paradise,
Shall arise and soar, from the snares of the world set free.'

This was what paradise meant for the Iranian people – to be rid of all the corruptions of the Shah and to 'arise and soar' into a new world. Now they felt it could be fulfilled.

## Sacrifice

But this was to be a costly freedom. Khomeini emphasized this repeatedly. This is a summary of one of his radio talks published in a newspaper:

'Our only basic reference is to the time of the prophet Mohammed and the Emam Ali. Look at all the sacrifices of the early prophets. Look at Moses – just one man called to fight against the corruptions of the Egyptians. Look at

Mohammed, our blessed prophet – everyone was against him; he had no weapon in his hand; he had to go underground and then one by one called his followers. At Medina he called on the people to rise against the enemy. It was an insurrection for God's sake. He had no weapons for his warfare (again and again he emphasized this). It was a revolution for God. It was the power of God that gave them strength. The power of faith was greater than the imperial power of Rome and of Iran in the seventh century. They did not allow their spirits to be broken. And you, my brothers, are part of this great country of Iran. You must protect this present revolution. This also is God's revolution. If our revolution is for God then there is no fear of martyrdom. If we kill it is paradise. If we are killed it is paradise. All of us must go forward together.'

Now I could understand why the people suffered so much. It was part of the great sacrifice of the prophet Mohammed and his family. All freedom was costly. That was why they were willing to close their shops for months on end and receive little income. They would queue all winter for a little paraffin, and freeze in their homes, to ensure the success of the oil fields strike against the Shah. Members of their families would mysteriously disappear, taken by the secret police, never to be seen again. This was part of the sacrifice.

One day we heard of terrible atrocities committed by the army in Najafobod, a suburb of Isfahan. Hundreds were killed; buildings were burnt. And yet, in face of opposition on this scale, the people did not give up. It was, as they saw it, a struggle for freedom – at any cost.

'The fountain falls when it reaches its height,' says the Persian proverb. The Shah had reached his height. He could go no higher. His fall, said the people, was inevitable.

The driver of the taxi in which I was sitting gesticulated wildly to show me how his son had been tortured and maimed by the secret police. Pictures of tortured people and dead bodies were displayed on many street walls in Isfahan. These were the victims of the secret police. One poster showed hundreds of dead bodies mown down by army gunfire on what they later called 'Black Friday'. I felt within my bones that it was the faith and solidarity of the people triumphing over the force of arms. In the words of one of the Psalms:

> 'I do not trust in my bow.
> My sword does not bring me victory.
> But thou has saved us from our foes.'

## Hussein the martyr

A little understanding of history helps us understand the Iranian thinking on martyrdom. More powerful even than the example of Mohammed was the suffering and martyrdom of his grandson Hussein. As an Arab he had married a Persian princess; this made him very special to Iranians. He was the greatest martyr of them all. He was the one who stood for freedom, truth and justice against the power of the enemy.

Every year, on the tenth day of the Arabic month of Muharram, the sacrifice of Hussein was celebrated throughout the country. I suppose our own Good Friday is the nearest equivalent. On that same date in the middle of the seventh century, in the heart of the desert at a place called Kerbala (in modern Iraq), Hussein and the seventy-two who were with him were surrounded by an army of 4,000 Arabs. He didn't have a chance. He and his small company were defenceless. They were not allowed water or food by the enemy. One of his relatives tried to get some water but the enemy killed him. Hussein's six-month-old son was butchered before his eyes. There was no one to come to their rescue.

The words of Mohammed's granddaughter, uttered at that time, could just as easily have been spoken in the early days of this revolution. She spoke out against Yazid, the tyrannical Arab leader who had attacked Hussein:

'O God Almighty, restore our rights, redress our grievances, and wreak vengeance on those who have perpetrated atrocity and tyranny against us. Pour your wrath on those who have shed our blood and torn our veils . . . praise be to God who has ordained martyrdom for his chosen ones and who has called them towards his mercy, kindness and paradise.'

This quotation was often in the newspapers and very much part of the current thinking. All the time Khomeini was drawing his inspiration from this period of history.

I vividly remember going with Parveez to the great covered bazaar of Isfahan to experience at first hand the way Muslims commemorate the anniversary of Hussein's martyrdom. This was a unique opportunity for me. Foreigners were warned to keep away as the presence of outsiders would not be welcome on such a fervently religious day (just as some Christians would not welcome a Muslim at a Good Friday service). I felt very conspicuous but Parveez, a man well-respected in the local community, assured me there was no danger. He and his friend, Ali Akbar, would protect me if there was any difficulty.

First we went to a meeting. All over the country, meetings like this were being held. We travelled by car. On this day every year there were no taxis in the streets, no music on the radio. The TV had only news bulletins. All cinemas were closed. Black flags hung from the door of every closed shop.

We arrived at a house with the meeting already in progress. It was so full of people that we had to sit outside and listen to a mullah speaking through a loud-speaker. He was recounting the tragic death of Hussein. All around us the people were weeping as they heard the horrors of that desert ordeal more than 1,200 years before.

We moved on to another house where again a mullah was

speaking. Here we were given *osh* (thick soup), which was also handed out to all the poor people. Parveez explained that this was the way they cared for all those who, like Hussein, had been deprived of the basic needs of life. My plate was filled high with this *osh* and although I didn't like it Ali Akbar told me I must eat it all up. I was glad to have some tea to wash it down!

Then we followed a big procession right through the covered bazaar towards the Friday mosque – the oldest one in Isfahan. The procession moved rhythmically to the sound of chanting and wailing. The young men had armed themselves with ropes and chains. They beat themselves with them, all the time calling out the name of Hussein. Others had mud on their heads and beat their bare breasts with their fists. I looked at the bruised body of one fairly old man. His shirt had been drawn down to his waist; his back was bleeding from the lashes of his rope. The women followed separately, all dressed in black and their heads covered with black veils. They too were crying and chanting the name of Hussein. I felt almost hypnotized by the rhythm of the singing and marching and the beating of the ropes and chains. The plight of Hussein and his seventy-two followers, with no bread or water, in the heat of that desert, was very real.

I asked Ali Akbar the meaning of the words they were chanting.

'We are saying to Hussein that we would have come to your rescue if we could have done,' he replied, 'but now we will join you in fighting for the truth . . . Hussein is the one who stood for the true religion against Yazid . . . it is the true religion we must all fight for.'

I recalled the description Bishop Dehqani gave us when we first arrived in Iran. He told us how, when he was young, he had joined his family and the village people and they had burnt the effigy of the hated Omar, the first caliph who conquered Iran. I now saw just how much this was a part of the lives of all the Iranian people.

Ali Akbar turned to me again.

'We must be free,' he said. 'Hussein died for the sake of freedom.'

I couldn't help thinking of the suffering of Jesus. Was this the kind of thing we as Christians should do on Good Friday? Jesus had died on the cross alone. He didn't have a single follower with him. At least Hussein had seventy-two companions.

Should we also say to Jesus:

'We would have come to your help when you suffered in that garden of Gethsemane. We would have saved you from that horrible death on the cross'?

But I knew in all honesty I could never say this. There was a great difference between the death of Jesus and of Hussein. I knew I must say:

'I would have killed you too, Jesus. The sin of those people was my sin too.'

As a Christian I believe it was the sin of us all that took Jesus to the cross.

'None is righteous, no, not one.'

There is evil in all of us, and it crucified him. And then I saw clearly that Jesus' suffering was not for himself, nor for him family and followers. It was for the very people who murdered him – for the evil in us all. It was *our* punishment he took on himself.

'The Lord has laid on him the sin of us all.'

He suffered so that I need not lash my body with ropes and chains. Through his cross I could find real forgiveness. It was his love for me that could stop me hating myself and hating others, even my enemies.

'By his stripes we are healed.'

The meaning of Jesus' sufferings and those of Hussein

seemed far apart on this understanding.

The day ended when we arrived at the Friday mosque. The atmosphere had changed. The procession had broken up. The wailing had ended. We were given afternoon tea consisting of free cigarettes, hot milk and more of that *osh*. I had been deeply moved and astounded by the depth of feeling I had experienced. Hussein's martyrdom was in the very blood of all these people. His willingness to suffer and to die was more powerful for them than the force of arms. Because of his martyrdom they knew that truth could prevail over power. On reflection I can understand that no one with me on that day in the bazaar of Isfahan would have been surprised that Iran could stage a revolution which would shake the world – a revolution that showed martyrdom as the way through to victory.

## The great revolutionary

Freedom for the poor; the fight against materialism; colonization (the word they constantly used to describe what the West had done to them); exploitation – these were the constant topics of conversation and of national news. A member of the staff of the university of Teheran, later a candidate for the Presidency, wrote a pamphlet (in Farsi) called 'The message of Jesus Christ'. He wrote as a Muslim who wanted to show that the life and teaching of Jesus were a direct challenge to the way of life in the West. This is a summary of what he wrote:

'The message of Christ opposes all that the capitalist West stands for. The very things that Emam Khomeini is saying repeat the words of Jesus. Jesus said, "we cannot serve God and Money"; "we must lay up for ourselves treasures in heaven and not on earth". He himself went into the temple and overturned the money tables of the rich. In the Sermon on the Mount he said that the kingdom belonged to the poor. When he came before Pilate at his trial it was in fact Pilate who was judged by Christ. Jesus was the great revolutionary. It was the capitalists, the rich people, the powerful, who tortured and killed him. Judas was the great traitor, and it is the people of the West who have betrayed Jesus. Come back to the message of Christ. Don't think all the time, as Jesus said, what you should be eating and drinking. Life is more than that. Jesus said he did not come to bring peace but the sword. Our battle, like Christ's, is against the imperialists, against the powerful and the rich.'

It seemed fascinating to me that a highly educated Muslim could write this.

Khomeini himself appealed to the ordinary people. One man described to me what he believed about the three rooms in which Khomeini lived in Qum, the holy city to the south of Teheran. One was his bedroom, one his study and one his reception room. The apparent simplicity of his lifestyle spoke very deeply to the masses.

A few months after Khomeini had returned to the country I went with a British friend to visit a farm about twenty miles outside Isfahan. My friend was helping to maintain the combine harvesters which had been imported from Britain. I talked with some of the men working on the farm. All of them supported the revolution.

'Look,' they said, 'our daily wages have risen since the *Aqa* came' (*Aqa,* meaning 'Sir', was the name the people often used when talking about Khomeini).

It really did seem that the poor were being helped in those early days of the revolution.

One day, reading the Persian newspaper, I was amazed to see the Methodist Church of the USA hit the front-page headlines. Apparently it had spoken out openly against the repression of the poor and was offering its solidarity to the oppressed in Iran. I was glad to find that the church was also being seen in this more positive light.

## Islamic Republic

How did we and our fellow missionaries react to all that was going on in the name of freedom and truth? A few days after Khomeini's return the bishop called a meeting of all the missionaries working with the church in Isfahan. There were about thirty of us. He felt it was important that we understood something of the meaning of the Islamic Republic. This was in fact the first one of its kind ever established. We needed to know what were the principles lying behind an Islamic state and how we could best witness for Christ in the new situation.

He helped us greatly to understand the thinking of Khomeini and those closest to him. He explained the great simplicity that was at the heart of the Muslims in Iran.

'The Muslims must obey God, the prophet Mohammed and the Emam. Every part of life is governed by God and for them this obviously must include politics and the whole of government. In this way the Ayatollah has authority over every part of national life.'

He pointed out the necessity of suffering for the truth, as Hussein had suffered at Kerbala.

'For them to obey the prophet is to obey God; to obey the Emam is to obey God; to obey the representative of the Emam (Khomeini) is to obey God.'

He showed us how, in this type of Islam, the religious leaders were the inheritors of the prophet, and therefore had power over the people and also over the king. This is why they had been able to overthrow the Shah, because their authority, from God, was greater than his. The Shah was ultimately answerable to God and to themselves as God's representatives.

We had some interesting discussion about the task of the Christians in this new situation.

'We are with the revolution against materialism, whether

it be capitalist or communist,' the bishop said. 'The important thing is that we are sincere – they will listen to us if we are.'

Only later did we realize that sincerity was not enough.

Bishop Dehqani talked also about being the light of the world and the salt of the earth.

'By who we are, much more than by what we say, we will show Christ to others,' he said. But he did not conceal the differences between Christianity and Islam:

'In Christianity the heart must be put right. In Islam it is through power that the state will act.'

## The cross

In this way we tried to see the revolution positively, and entered with some hope into its first birth-pangs of joyous freedom.

We were disillusioned all too quickly. Arastoo Sayyah was murdered. How could we see this atrocious deed in terms of freedom, justice and truth? The bishop publicly stated that Arastoo's martyrdom was the Christian contribution to the cause of the revolution. Who then were the murderers?

'They were counter-revolutionaries,' said the chief mullah in Shiraz, 'and all of us must unite against them on behalf of the ideals of the revolution.'

One thing was clear, both for the revolution and for the church. Truth and suffering for the truth went hand in hand. Thousands had been killed in their support for the revolution. Now our tiny church, through the martyrdom of its senior pastor, had taken its share in the suffering. It too was counting the cost of freedom and truth.

My wife, Diana, caught a glimpse of the joining together of pain and truth in a letter she wrote at Easter, just a month after Arastoo's murder:

'With the combination of Arastoo's death and Easter, I

felt we were having to trust more and understand less. Jesus, and even Arastoo, had to leave this earth when they were really fruitful in their ministry. It came over so clearly that Jesus, at the point of great pain, even death, trusted the love and plan of his Father. Somehow, to hold together pain which we don't understand (either of adjustment, upheaval or death) and trust in the love of God who has planned it – this is a uniquely Christian hope which gives me great comfort.'

How much had Arastoo stood for the truth? This morning before writing this paragraph, I received a letter from Jane Austin, who worked for ten years as a nurse at the Christian hospital in Shiraz. Arastoo was her pastor. She knew him well. She writes of the warmth of his love for people. On one occasion she remembers that he spoke in an unusual way for an Iranian:

'I remember that once he preached on the evils of bargaining – something which most of his congregation accepted without thought, as they had been brought up with it. He pointed out that in fact it was a form of lying, as both the seller and the customer knew the true value of the article and yet were lying to each other in the hope of gaining advantage.'

I often think of that cross standing on the top of the domed roof of the church in Shiraz. Arastoo would first talk with a young inquirer inside the church before taking him or her outside and pointing up to the dome. Then he would show the cross. He never tried to hide it. For him the cross was the way to the heart of God. It was the key to life itself. It was for this belief that he was murdered.

## Whisky or tea?

I had a hard time with my young Muslim friends in the copper-engraving shop in these months.

'Death to the Shah,' they said in unison as I entered the shop a few days after Khomeini had returned.

'Go on, you say it too,' they urged. 'The Shah is Satan. Death to the Shah,' they repeated.

I knew I was in a difficult position. I told them as a Christian I could not say this.

'Only God,' I said, 'can judge the evil of men. Each of us has a bit of good and a bit of evil. I must answer to God for the bad that is in me, not the bad that may be in the Shah.'

They were very quiet when I gave this answer. They never asked me again to join in their slogans.

Another day, in March 1979, I went to see Mehran, a friend who owned a small shoe shop near the bazaar. We had met each other first on the mountain walk and he had invited me to his shop to drink tea with him. Then he invited Diana and me to his home. We sat on the floor, his wife placed the food on the table cloth in front of us and we ate the supper. He even produced some whisky! From this I realized he was a more liberal kind of Muslim than my other friends. Later he invited me to his other house where he had a second wife. He told me that sometimes he would stay in one house and sometimes in the other. Apparently the wives never met each other! One day he came to our house and gave us a demonstration of how to cook kebab on an open charcoal fire.

I was rather glad to meet a Muslim who wasn't afraid to drink even though he didn't have the courage to buy it for himself! Strictly speaking, of course, it is forbidden to him in the Qur'an. At least I felt he was being true to himself and not trying to pretend in front of me.

But that day when I went to see him he told me he wasn't drinking alcohol any more. When I next visited his house the whisky had disappeared. We drank tea. Somehow I felt he had lost something of his identity.

'To be a mullah is easy;
to be a man is difficult,'
runs the Persian proverb.

Mehran was having to pretend again. I knew he liked an occasional drink. Now he had to act as if he didn't.

## Intimidation

It was a hot Friday afternoon, 19 August 1979. I was having a Farsi lesson in my study. Demetri, the church administrator, knocked hastily on the door and came in.

'They've invaded the bishop's house and the church offices,' he said. 'You must go over there quickly.'

My teacher, a very gentle and polite Iranian, seemed even more astonished at this news than I was. I apologized to him for ending the lesson early and rushed over.

Margaret, the bishop's wife, was standing on the verandah of the house.

'Thirty men came in. They went through all the rooms ... ransacked everything ... they took our photos, our precious visitors' book, and other personal belongings ...'

Apparently these ruffians, young and middle-aged, bearded and unbearded, had knocked gently at the gate, and when it had been half-opened had savagely forced their way in. They didn't say who they were or who had sent them. They had also looked over all the books in the bishop's study, and even asked him why he had so many about Islam. He told them that a Christian had a duty to learn about the Islamic faith!

I went over to the church offices. The Financial Secretary was there. Tears rolled down his face as I met him. Filing cabinets in his office had been forced open and a bonfire made of all the contents. Years of work had been destroyed in a few minutes. I could smell the burning paper in the yard outside. He felt utterly shocked and horrified. They didn't allow anyone to use the telephone while they were doing all this damage. Immediately they had all left, the bishop rang the number he had been given only the day before by a revolutionary guard. They expressed surprise and regret and wanted to know who the people were. One of them had been recognized and so the bishop gave his name.

The whole affair left a bitter taste in my mouth. It really seemed that law and order had broken down. There was no one who could show any kind of authority against this kind of intimidation and aggression.

It was evident that the Government was in no way officially responsible for what was happening. The problem was that the central Government had little control over local Revolutionary Councils, and therefore was unable to do anything when this kind of illegal action took place. Already the Christian hospitals in Isfahan and Shiraz had been illegally taken over. A school for blind boys, run by German missionaries for many years, had also been occupied just one week before. All these take-overs were treacherous acts with no conceivable basis in justice or honesty.

## Arrest

The bishop, as leader of the church, felt that at every point a strong protest should be made both to Khomeini and to the Prime Minister's office. He sought the constant advice of his lawyer – a Muslim. At the possible risk of his own life the lawyer encouraged the bishop to protest in the name of justice against all that was being done illegally. He argued that one day law and order would return to the country and then the protests would be on record for all to see. Later the bishop was to write a letter to *The Times* newspaper in Britain, in which he quoted an Islamic saying:

'A state can live without belief, not without justice.'

The Muslim lawyer could see the truth of this too.

I had written down some words spoken by the bishop in a sermon a few years before. Now they leapt up at me from the page.

'Love for God demands truth. It faces the tension and does not acquiesce in evil.'

He was now putting his sermon into action. This took a lot of courage. These protests could endanger his life.

Six weeks later (8 October 1979) the bishop's courage was to be further tested. It was the day before we were to move to Teheran, where I had been appointed pastor to the Persian- and English-speaking congregations. We had packed everything and the lorry was due to arrive that afternoon. Bishop Dehqani and Margaret had invited us to lunch. It was a kind of farewell occasion.

Margaret met us at the door.

'They've arrested him,' she said.

We were shocked. Would this mean we were never to see him again? Any words we had seemed to evaporate. We knew that, the day before, a man who said he was from the Revolutionary Court in Shiraz had come to the bishop demanding payment of the money the hospital had sent to the central church funds over the past ten years. This was an incredible demand. The bishop had tried his best to explain that he was only the trustee of the fund and that the money belonged to the church. It certainly did not belong to the group who had illegally taken over the hospital in Shiraz.

That same day the man had returned to the bishop, bringing with him a piece of paper from the local Revolutionary Council. Two revolutionary guards were with him, and also the head of the hospital in Shiraz, an Iranian Christian, who had been put in prison but now seemed to be released. They again demanded that he pay over the money. The bishop once more explained that it was not his money – it belonged to the church. In fact he explained concisely that

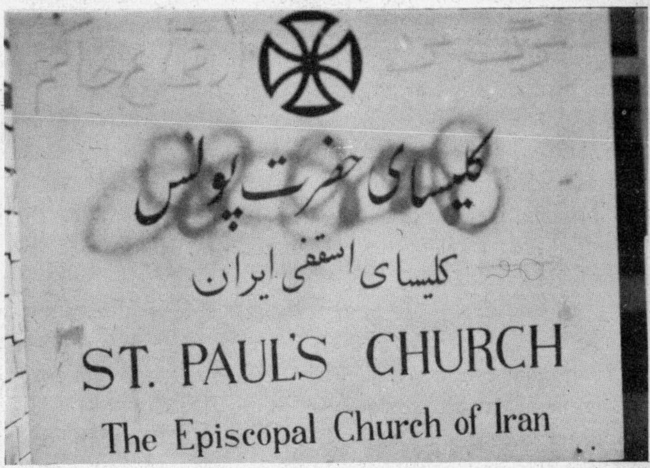


The defaced notice-board of St Paul's Church, Teheran, where Paul Hunt became pastor for his last few months in Iran. Any notice-board anywhere is open to this kind of abuse, but opposition to the Anglican church ran very deep in Iran at that time.

every institution belonging to the church paid a small percentage of its annual income to the central trust fund of the church. This money was used to pay for things like the salaries of the clergy and the pensions of over 120 workers. And so in no way had he any authority to hand it over.

It was then that they took him. He was driven away dressed as he was in his purple cassock and wearing his cross.

We sat down to lunch. Margaret asked me to sit in the bishop's chair. His place seemed so very empty. The Christian doctor from the hospital in Shiraz sat with us. Somehow he seemed to be involved in all that was happening to the bishop, but nothing was very clear. Margaret must have felt an enormous strain. The amazing thing was that she could still be the perfect hostess, despite not knowing what they might do to her husband. At lunch she told us that what was happening would lead to the deeper growth of the church. Later I heard that when she said goodbye to the bishop she said to him:

'I am very proud of you that you are able to stand up for the truth.'

Later that evening I rang up the bishop's house. To my delight I heard his voice. The sense of relief was overwhelming. He told me that for five hours he had been detained, and for one of those was locked in a small cell. He said how in that ordeal he had been brought closer to God than ever before. He too did not know if he would be released. The Sunday before, in the church service which he had attended, I had been speaking about the storm on the sea of Galilee when Jesus was asleep in the boat. I had used some words from an English mystic writer who had written that it is in the storms of life that we begin to know the reality of Christ; without the storms we do not experience his great power. These words had been a great help to the bishop in that time of solitary confinement. He too had experienced the deep peace of Christ, and been upheld in the storm by the amazing power of God.

Later we learned how he had been released. Demetri, the church administrator, had gone immediately to the Governor General's office. Although the Govenor General was in a meeting Demetri insisted that word be taken to him that Bishop Dehqani had been arrested. He said that if the bishop was not released immediately the fact would very soon be out in the international news. The Governor General sensed the danger of the situation. He ordered the immediate release of the bishop. Demetri had risked his own life in doing what he did. But his loyalty to his bishop and to God came first.

A few days later, the bishop talked to our congregation in Teheran. He quoted some words that an old caretaker of his garden, who was a Muslim, had said to him following this experience:

'I thank God that you stood up for truth and honesty, because that helps Islam and our revolution.'

'This,' added the bishop, 'is part of the meaning of the cross – being ready to stand up for love of the truth.'

# 8

# MISSIONARY GO HOME!

It was the day after the Shah had left the country. I went to buy some bread in the small bakery by the mosque just down the road. A group of young men looked at me inquisitively as I walked past. They seemed a bit aggressive. I stopped.

'Why are you still here?' they asked.

It was a natural enough question. Most foreigners had either left or were preparing to leave. I wasn't sure how to answer them immediately. I mouthed some polite Persian phrases.

'Why don't you go home?' they said.

I told them I was a priest and that my work for God continued, whatever happened. I pointed to the church door to show where I lived.

'In our country we have many of your mullahs,' I told them, 'so in this country the Christians have priests.'

It still didn't sound convincing to them.

'I want to stay here,' I said. 'I love your country and I try to pray each day for the revolution.'

It was this last remark that got through to them. They smiled. The language of prayer was their language too. The call to prayer had just been sounded from the mosque behind us. We shook hands and I left them.

'Why are you staying on?'

It was a question we often asked ourselves as the revolution gained in momentum. Two months later we had the annual meeting for the clergy. In the middle of one of the discussions one of my fellow Iranian pastors turned to me.

'And why are you still here?' he asked.

I hope our reasons become clear to the reader by the end of this chapter.

## Wanted?

There was no doubt that the missionaries had been instrumental in building the Iranian church. Dr Robert Bruce, a member of our own missionary society, had been one of the founder members of the church a hundred years before.

I remember the moment when we first arrived at the airport customs. The face of the customs official lit up when I told him we were going to live next to the Christian hospital in Isfahan.

'I owe my life to Dr Schafter,' he said, speaking of a British doctor who had worked there thirty years before.

Once, in a village, I talked with a man who was throwing the wheat against a sieve to separate it from the chaff. He was another who would never forget the Christian hospital in Isfahan and the prayers which he used to attend when he was a patient. It was through the hospital belonging to the church in Yazd that Bishop Dehqani's mother had become a Christian. Although his father remained a Muslim, his mother's influence prevailed and he became a Christian.

As we settled into life in Isfahan we too found that people were very welcoming. Once a shopkeeper asked Diana who her husband was.

'He's a priest in the church,' she said.

'Oh, he must be a spiritual man; that's good. I'll give you a reduction!' he replied.

And so when the hospital was suddenly seized in early June, the words the bishop sent through Jean Waddell echoed what many felt.

'I hope very much that you are all in good heart and not feeling rejected or unwanted. I can assure you that you are certainly not unwanted in any way by the people you have served.'

That was certainly a real part of how people felt. They knew that the missionaries had come to serve God and the Iranians, and they were grateful for them.

## Motley crew

We were a strange mixture of people working in the one team under the leadership of the bishop. The church consisted of different institutions. In a Muslim country the way our church had chosen to show the love of Christ was through the hospitals, the schools, work with the blind, and hostels for boys and girls. About thirty missionaries were involved in these, mostly in Isfahan.

Some of the missionaries were Dutch, working on a farm about twenty miles outside Isfahan. They trained blind men from the villages. After six months or so of training, a blind man would return to his own village, able to do a job of work in the fields. He need no longer sit at home doing nothing. He had been trained in this way. Nothing else like this work existed in Iran.

Sometimes I went with Jan, one of the Dutchmen, to a village for a day. We would talk quietly with some of the people and tell them about the training farm. Slowly we would find out if there were any blind men in that village. This would always take time, as the villagers were ashamed to admit that they did have blind people. Then we would find the home where a blind man was living. We talked with the family, telling them that the farm might be just the right place for their son. Jan would return several more times, and finally gain their trust. It was work involving great patience and a knowledge of the way the villagers' minds worked.

Then there were two or three German families in charge of a blind school for boys, called Christofel. Mr Christofel, himself a German, had started the work over fifty years before. Gerhard, a particular friend of mine, was the head of the school when the revolution came. He often asked me to go and speak to the boys at their daily prayers. These were voluntary, as they didn't want to force any boy to become a Christian, but usually between fifteen and twenty would attend.

Felix was another of the Germans working there. He and I always spoke to each other in Persian, as I didn't know German and he didn't know English! Every Sunday Gerhard or Felix would bring a big car full of the blind boys to the church service. The boys knew the Persian hymns by heart and loved the Bible stories. One of them later wanted to be ordained and our church sent him to train at a theological college in India.

There was also a Christian bookshop very close to the

church. Lief, a Danish missionary, was in charge of this. It sold books of all kinds, especially Christian ones, to Iranians and to foreigners.

The Christian hospital was often called the 'British' hospital by the local taxi drivers and others. This was a great pity, as all the workers, except a few doctors and nurses, were Iranians or came from India or Pakistan. But certainly the British influence had been very great and the head of the hospital had always been from England. For many years it had been the only hospital in Isfahan. Now there were at least ten others, but many Iranians still preferred to go to the Christian hospital, as they felt that the medical service and the care given to the patients there was the best. In the last years of the Shah a completely new building had been erected. There were also clinics in two or three villages where the hospital staff went each week.

At the girls' home for the blind, called Noor Ayin ('the way of light'), British missionaries had been working for a long time. Many Iranians think it degrading to work with blind people. For this reason it was always difficult to find the right type of people to take over this kind of work. Margaret and Elizabeth, our friends who worked there, had to be willing to put their hands to anything – cleaning snow from the roofs, unblocking the drains and keeping the very old central heating system going (it was always leaking!), as well as all the care for the blind girls and the Iranian helpers.

Brian and Marianna, a young couple who had first met each other in Iran, were in charge of a hostel for boys. Brian was English and Marianna German. An American student worked with them. They lived with a small number of boys, and through the daily life of the hostel they tried to show something of God's love.

Elizabeth was in charge of a similar hostel for girls. She really loved them and each day she led prayers with them and tried to understand their needs.

There were also seven young volunteers who came to Isfahan for a period of two years to help in the hostels and the hospital – they came to help, but in fact, like us all, they received at least as much as they gave.

Dutch, Germans, Danes, British – yes, we were a motley crew trying to work together in a fairly small church. There were other missionaries working in the Christian hospital in Shiraz and in bookshop and school work in Teheran. Dr John Coleman and his wife, Audrey, worked at a clinic in Yazd, a large desert city in the centre of Iran.

## Guns and ointment

All this work was appreciated. But there was another side to it as well.

'I hate you because I need you,' were the exact words used about the missionaries by a Christian Iranian. At the farm for the blind, Iranians took over the work from the Dutch. But in all the other institutions the missionaries were still needed. But the people who were needed were the same people who were hated.

Hate might seem a strong word. But I think it is the right one. Where there is true love there is also hate. Otherwise the love is not real. Perhaps this strange mixture will be more comprehensible if I speak from personal experience. I came as a Westerner to Iran. I don't feel that I am a very powerful person. I wasn't even in charge of one of the institutions of the church. But I did represent the powerful West; the West with all its know how, with all its feeling of superiority.

'Whether you know it or not, you as a Westerner make me feel inferior,' said that same Iranian Christian to me.

I vividly remember the bishop explaining to the volunteers who had recently arrived from England some of the difficulties which they, as foreigners, would meet in their work with Iranians.

'The Westerners come with all the power and the efficiency,' he said, 'but the gospel you bring is all about the cross and the true meaning of suffering and the right kind of weakness.'

He went on to explain that this was a big problem, for how does something that is seen to be powerful bring a message which is its exact opposite. I knew, for myself, that if anyone did understand anything about Christ through me it was very much in spite of what I was. For we, as missionaries, were those who came with all the power of the West behind us. We were the ones expected to show authority and leadership. Yes we were needed; some people even loved us. But we were hated too – or at least resented.

In fact it was, in miniature, everything that the British Empire had meant to the world in the previous century.

'The gun and the ointment came together when the colonialists came.'

I had heard a Japanese theologian say this at a meeting I had attended in Malaysia some years before.

'You Westerners brought the ointment – the healing – but you brought us the gun as well, and we couldn't have the one without the other.'

I was now experiencing something of the meaning of what he had said. Perhaps we as missionaries had been more aware of the ointment, but others had seen things differently.

## Agents of imperialism

Deep down we also knew that the church was very Persian. Our Bishop was an Iranian. All five clergy were Iranians. Often at Christmas time I remember the Iranian hospital evangelist, at the hospital prayers, saying that Jesus was an Easterner and not from the West – that Christianity was truly Eastern. The wise men, he said, came from the East looking for their king. They found him in Jesus. I knew from church history that the ancient Persian church had been one of the greatest missionary churches ever to exist. They sent Persian missionaries to India and even as far as China.

The bishop would often remind us that Christians are God's people, irrespective of nationality.

'Let the people see the foreigners come to the English-speaking service,' he would say. 'It's a very good witness for Christ.'

And so it was. One Christmas I counted twelve different nationalities in the choir, including Iranians. It was a unity we shared together in Christ.

And yet, inevitably, there were suspicions. If we were foreigners, why were we there? Betty Gurney, for forty years a missionary in Iran, once told us how her husband, David, got to know a mullah. The relationship grew over several years. It was a good friendship. One day the mullah took him on one side.

'Tell me the truth,' he said. 'What are you really doing this work for?'

David tried to explain his love for Christ and the gospel.

'But surely you have another reason,' said the mullah.

He could not believe this was the sole reason for David's presence.

Khomeini, in the *Little Green Book* which he wrote in exile before returning to Iran, doesn't hide his real feelings about foreign missionaries.

'Western missionaries, carrying out secret plans drawn up centuries ago, have created religious schools of their own within Muslim countries. We did not react against that, and this is what it led to. These missionaries infiltrated our villages and our countryside to turn our children into Christians or atheists . . . they have been aware ever since the Crusades that only Islam with its laws and its faith can bar the way to their material interests and political power. The missionaries, as agents of imperialism, are also busy throughout the Muslim world in perverting our youth – not by converting them to their own religion but by corrupting them. In Teheran itself propaganda centres for Christianity, Zionism and Baha'i have been set up for the sole purpose of luring the faithful away from the commandments of Islam. Is it not our duty to destroy all these sources of danger to Islam?'

Whether we liked it or not, we Western missionaries came increasingly under suspicion as the revolution gained ground. For the Muslim, religion and politics are very closely bound together. And so they assumed that our religion in the same way was closely involved with politics. To them it was natural that someone like me would have political motives. I often tried to explain that my work was simply to teach the Bible to those who wanted to learn, to pray and to lead the worship in church. But this seemed too simple to some of them.

## Spy base

I asked Parveez one day what he thought about the take-over of the Christian hospital. His own life had been saved in that hospital by Dr Schafter, and he had always talked about him with great affection. His own daughters had their children in the hospital.

'If they are spies then they must suffer for it,' he said.

Parveez, a man who had received so much from the missionary doctors and nurses, felt that they might well be Western spies. Such was the propaganda of the revolution.

At the time the hospital was seized the national newspaper had these headlines:

'British hospital seized; proclaimed a spy base.'

It then continued: 'In an announcement, the Islamic

Revolutionary Court said the hospital was a "first class spy base of the West". According to witnesses and evidence produced before the court it was proved that the hospital was a spying den of the foreigners against the Iranian masses, the court said. Disclosing the evidence placed before the Islamic court the announcement said that the hospital building was constructed by Iranians against whom documentary proof had been gathered proving them to be spies and loyal to the foreigners ... the hospital was not only an abuse to Jesus Christ but was converted into an anti-Islamic operations centre; it was a propaganda base aiming to mislead our youth, the court charged. The court accused the hospital administrators of mismanagement, spending vast sums of money for anti-Islamic propaganda, for the construction of useless buildings, and for the purchase of unnecessary equipment.'

We were all utterly amazed at the charges. It was possible that zealous Muslims could find the preaching of the gospel a real threat, but we knew the other charges were totally baseless. No real evidence was produced for these accusations.

Professor Lambton, a great authority on Iran, wrote a letter to *The Times* newspaper pointing out that in past history, particularly in the late thirteenth century, the church in Iran had suffered murders, intimidations and false accusation. Now, she wrote:

'There is a new and ugly addition to the accusations made against the Christians, namely that of spying.'

She goes on to say that any contact between local and foreign Christians almost automatically arouses suspicion.

This certainly happened in my own case. Three months after leaving Iran I was officially accused of handing over $500 million and 300 kilos of TNT explosives to counter-revolutionaries, on behalf of the CIA and British Intelligence.

I was astounded. If people believe that of us, they can believe anything!

Of course you can always look back and say:

'If only the church hadn't got all those missionaries. If only the institutions had not been so dependent on Westerners.'

But I believe that is to deny the realities of the situation. I can say quite unashamedly that the missionaries brought much good to the people of Iran. Yet it was almost impossible to do so without being misunderstood. People always saw us as representing the powerful West.

## Kicked out

I shall never forget the meeting of missionaries that took place the day after the hospital had been taken over by the Revolutionary Council and the British staff told never to enter the hospital again. It was our usual Wednesday evening gathering when we met for prayer and for studying the Bible. We were all bewildered. After nearly a hundred years the hospital had suddenly been seized. Here were doctors and nurses who had worked there for five, ten, or fifteen years. They had been kicked out. They were without a job. Everything they had built up – the new buildings, the equipment, the relationships with the staff, above all the love of Christ they had tried to show – had all been violently rejected.

Jackie, one of the nurses, led the meeting. She quoted a verse from the Bible:

'Be still and know that I am God.'

We tried to be still, numbed by the shock of what had happened. We needed to know that God was truly with us. Then one of the other nurses said she felt that through what was happening we were beginning to learn something about humility; we had a lot of pride that God needed to deal with.

Rupert, a surgeon, felt too shattered to say much. He had heard a local carpenter saying that all the things that were wrong with the country were 'everyone else's fault'. Rupert felt we can too easily say 'it's all their fault', without seeing that it may be ours as well.

Brigid, another nurse, spoke up. She had the keys to the stores. She was asked to hand them over. Everything in her wanted to throw them into the river, but then she realized how Christ's reaction would have been to give the keys and even to show them what was in the stores.

'I need to come back again and again to the cross and say, "Father, forgive,"' she said.

Margaret, another member of the group, remembered how Jesus, facing his own rejection, knew what was coming to him but could still love those who rejected him.

We all confessed to finding in ourselves an increasing distrust of others. I said that when someone knocked at our door we now immediately became distrustful and apprehensive. People around us seemed to be becoming paranoid, trusting no one, and we were catching this fear. Someone else in the group urged us not to take the hatred too personally. It may not be directed at a particular missionary, but just part of a general hatred against all foreigners.

Diana reflected that we can only forgive when we know how much we ourselves are personally loved by our heavenly Father. Jesus, on the cross, was loved by God so much more than he was hated by men. With such love he could say: 'Father, forgive'.

I felt that God was working deeply in our lives through what was happening. Maybe it took something like this to open us up in a fresh way to the meaning of forgiveness. Some words I once read in a parish magazine have always remained in my mind:

'God has more to do in you than through you.'

He was certainly doing a lot in us.

## Why stay?

Slowly the exodus of missionaries did take place. Those seven young volunteers were the first to leave. Jan and his wife and family left with them. Then the hospital staff went. I watched Dr Pont's car leaving in the early dawn of a hot summer morning. For fifteen years he had given his life to the hospital. Now he and his wife, Molly, their lives already threatened, were being forced out. Sue, who had been their main stalwart in the hospital for those years, had gone on holiday a little before, hoping to return. She never did. Two other couples, the wives pregnant, decided to leave.

Soon after, the boys' blind school was seized. I was there one morning taking the prayers. Gerhard told me that twelve armed men had come in earlier and ordered them to leave within seventy-two hours. For some days previously he had sat down with the group who wanted to take it over and tried to talk with them. But talk was useless. Now for those three days the guards watched their every movement. They had time to gather what they could into suitcases. The Muslim group moved in to take it over.

The three women missionaries at the girls' blind school were able to stay on, but in great uncertainty. Each day they felt it might also be taken over. John Coleman, who had also been ordained, and I, were the last foreign clergy to remain.

Why did Diana and I stay on at this time?

Put simply, our job of work was still there. The missionaries who left only went when their work was taken from them. We were due to move to Teheran so that I could work at St Paul's Church. We felt it would be right for us to leave if our work was taken from us, if the church said they no longer wanted foreign clergy, or if our work permits were not renewed by the government.

We knew how important it was to be flexible – ready to go or stay, whichever God wanted. We prayed that God would guide us and that if he wanted us to go he would make this clear – perhaps by letting our work permits be refused or by a complete exodus of foreigners (which never happened). Or if we met a gunman we would leave – but this was an extraordinary idea: something we never thought would happen.

Nothing is more vital than knowing that God's will is more important than anything else. We somehow felt that if he called us to stay he would give us strength to live with whatever happened. And this was why, despite tremendous pressure to leave from our families and friends, we knew it was right to remain. But it was like living in a street scheduled for demolition, where everyone else had left except you. How would you feel?

One of our greatest supports in all this time was the Church Missionary Society to which we belonged. Olive Hitchcock was the one responsible for the missionaries working in Iran and other parts of the Middle East. It was she who constantly kept in touch with the parents and families of all the missionaries. She gave us all much encouragement.

At the height of our fears in the revolution she wrote to the missionaries in Iran:

'I am sure the element of fear is one if the most difficult things to deal with, and this is a very testing situation for all Christians who have to acknowledge their fears along with their faith and trust in God, and it makes the faith and trust more real. The way you are able to comfort and help each other must make a big difference, and it is a comfort to us to know you are not isolated and that you have between you tremendous inner resources.'

Olive was to feel the pain of the revolution as deeply as anyone. It was no easy task for her to communicate with the family of the missionaries who were in Iran, to keep them informed and to try to explain to some angry relatives why we were all still there.

As the storm gathered over the church we knew the coming days would be full of uncertainty. We knew too that we could experience the truth of some words Olive wrote:

'Putting your foot down in a mist and finding it on a rock.'

So, in October 1979, we moved to Teheran.

# 9
# THE EYE OF THE STORM

The telephone rang at 7 a.m. on our first morning in Teheran. My Iranian colleague sounded excited.

'Your car's been painted red,' he said. 'Come quickly.'

I rushed downstairs. He was right. Red paint had been splashed all over it, and the gate and door of our house had been covered with red paint too.

I felt apprehensive. The strange thing was that the car next to ours, belonging to the church caretaker, a Muslim, was totally untouched. All kinds of questions arose in my mind. Was it an inside job? Who had given the tip-off that a new pastor had come to the church? Was it just a prank, or did it have a deeper meaning?

An Iranian Christian from Shiraz was staying in the flat immediately above ours. He didn't ease my mind when he said to me:

'Red – the colour of blood.'

It was all right for him. That afternoon he returned home.

The position was that the previous pastor, an Iranian called Khalil, had left St Paul's church a few months before. His life had been threatened several times. He had received a menacing letter, and some phone calls. His Australian wife had returned to her country with their children earlier in the year. He was torn in two. Should he stay with his church or join his family? Finally he left. A few days later the revolutionary guards took his car, refusing to let me use it unless Khalil came back in person and reported to them.

Then, in the early summer, the bishop invited me to take Khalil's place and be in charge of the Persian- and English-speaking congregations at St Paul's – the Anglican church in Teheran. As foreigners, our position was easier than that of an Iranian pastor. Our lives had never been threatened, and we would be much safer just because we were not Iranians.

Two days after our arrival there was a row between our caretaker's family and one of the Iranian Christian families. I was called in to mediate. There were loud arguments, tears and many threats. There seemed no way through it all. And yet after two hours some kind of mutual understanding was reached. According to custom, the two men kissed each other as a sign of friendship. It was the Muslim caretaker who went first to the Christian and kissed him.

## Miracle

Three weeks later, on the morning of Friday 26 October 1979, we were in the middle of our English-speaking service. Diana was hastily called out of the church. Jean Waddell, the bishop's secretary, was on the phone. She returned a few minutes later and handed me a message.

'Early this morning there was an attempt on the bishop's life, but he is alive and well.'

I stopped the service. It seemed right to share this news with the congregation and to give thanks to God for such a deliverance.

Immediately after the service I phoned the bishop in Isfahan.

Bishop Dehqani-Tafti, with his wife Margaret and daughters Shireen and Guli, reunited in London after Bahram's assassination. The bishop had flown in from his conference in Cyprus; his wife and daughters from Iran.

'I shouldn't really be speaking to you now,' he said. 'It's a miracle I'm alive.'

In the next few days we slowly put together all the different parts of the story. Early that morning three armed men had gained access to the bishop's garden by climbing over a wall and on to the roof of the offices next door. One of the men held at gunpoint the bishop's step-brother and wife, who lived in a separate small house. Two others mounted the outside stairs leading to the bedroom. They opened the door.

'*Oskof*' ('bishop'), said one of them.

'*Bali, bali*' ('yes, yes'), said the bishop, as he woke from his light sleep.

From only two feet away, the man then fired five shots at the bishop's head.

'At that distance,' said Margaret Dehqani later, 'you couldn't miss even if you'd never had a gun in your hand before.'

The astounding thing is that they did miss. Not one shot hit the bishop's head. Four bullets ripped into the pillow; one hit Margaret's left hand as she flung herself across to shield her husband.

She then chased the gunmen down the stairs and to the other end of the garden, shouting at them and asking why they had done this. A piece of scrap metal had already been placed against the wall and they managed to escape into the early morning darkness.

This is how the bishop later described it when he spoke on the radio in England:

'They came to our room and fired five shots at my head, round my head and my wife's, and injured my wife. It happened so quickly that when I saw the barrel of the gun and the firing went on, I felt very ... in a way ... light. I felt, "Well, there's the end now. My responsibilities are finished as far as this world is concerned." And the feeling of fear wasn't there at all, and I really mean it. So much so that when I felt my head and came out of it and nothing had happened, again my shoulders felt the heaviness of responsibility. In a way it's more difficult to live all the time under pressure than to die in a moment. Death is really not all that frightening if one believes. To live under pressure is more difficult.'

It was obviously a carefully planned attempt to assassinate him. Apparently one man went to the Christian hospital, a little after the gunmen had been, to ask for the bishop's body. He was astounded to hear he was very much alive!

Margaret later said how it felt as if a 'blanket of prayer' had surrounded them at that fateful moment. Was it just a coincidence the bishop had not been killed? But who could miss at that range? Was there not a force at work greater than anything man can do?

We later found out that a few hours before the assassination attempt a meeting of people belonging to our missionary society took place in Ramsgate, on the Kentish coast, in England. The meeting heard reports from Uganda and Iran, including parts of a letter from Bishop Dehqani. It seemed right at that point to break for a short time of prayer in groups of three or four.

'Soon there was a buzz of prayer,' reported one of the people there. 'It went on, sometimes dying down, then welling up again. The name "Dehqani" could be heard repeatedly. No one knew that the bishop would be in particular danger that night but there seemed an urgency about the prayer and there was a reluctance to return from it to the rest of the meeting.'

Who can tell what the force of prayer can do?

I went to Teheran airport two days later to meet the bishop and Margaret. He spoke at the Persian church service on Sunday evening, describing what had happened. We saw the pillowcase with those four bullet holes. Margaret's left hand was in plaster. Only the word 'miracle' is adequate to describe such an escape.

In the same week, a meeting of church leaders took place in Teheran. Bishop Dehqani spoke:

'Either we stand for the truth and are willing to be killed – the way of the cross,' he said, 'or we are cautious and are wiped out.'

These were not just idle words. He was living by them.

The following day he left Iran to visit other churches in the Middle East. This visit had been planned for many months. He told us all that in six weeks he would return. A suitcase was the only luggage he took with him. In fact, with the storm gathering, he was not to return at all.

## At home

In the next months, although we were faced with much uncertainty, our daily life continued much as usual. Between thirty and fifty Iranians came to our Sunday evening church services, and on Friday mornings British, Americans, Indians and Pakistanis gathered for worship in English. We felt the atmosphere in the streets was freer than in Isfahan. Diana felt less conspicuous as a foreign woman because there were other foreigners around. Also many Iranian women dressed in Western style. In the local shops people were friendly. Often they would say:

'It's the American and British governments we don't like, but we have no quarrel with their people.'

Diana transformed our flat into a real home. As a family we decided to be as settled as we could, so she bought curtains and we put up pictures.

'All nappies and noses,' was how she once described her life as a mum with a three-year-old and a one-year-old to contend with.

One day we were crossing the main road that runs north-south through the heart of Teheran. A small Iranian boy had just given Rosemary an enormous, orange balloon. She was thrilled with it. We set out on the rather perilous journey across the six lanes of traffic. A gust of wind snatched the balloon from her small, outstretched hands, and a little English girl, in the middle of all the cars, stood with tears pouring down her face. Happily that wasn't the end of the story. An Iranian on the far side of the road saw what had happened, retrieved the balloon, and held it triumphantly in the air. The cars actually stopped while I recrossed the road, watched anxiously by Rosemary. They waited until the precious thing was in her hands again. Many of them were smiling. Just a few moments, a mixture of ordinary happiness and sorrow, such as could happen in any street, in any town. But it showed something of the friendliness of the people.

In fact our two children helped us a lot to see the lighter side of life. When the Shah was still in power, Rosemary had learnt to pronounce his name with great pride and confidence. It was one of the first words she learnt. She would come with us into a shop, see his picture and shout out 'Shah, Shah'. Then we had to re-educate her! The word 'Khomeini' was much more difficult for a three-year-old to say! But she managed it. Often the atmosphere would change in a shop when she pointed to the revered picture of the Ayatollah and pronounced his name. Just once or twice, to our embarrassment, she let slip the wrong name! But children can be forgiven many things.

We regularly took Rosemary to the swings and slides at the bottom of our street, near the centre of the city. She played happily with the Iranian children and even learnt some Farsi. Her fair hair was always an attraction, yet it also made her more conspicuous. I chatted quite a bit with students who gathered there. One of them talked with me about my job and called me the 'God worshipper'! I remember another one saying it would take a hundred years to get the country right after all that it had been through.

## Light in the dark

Early in November the US Embassy was suddenly attacked and the hostages taken. We felt deeply for the Americans held captive, but we could also understand something of the anger of Iranians who felt exploited and dominated by the West. However, no one troubled our American friends – teachers and missionaries living in Teheran. One of them told me that in his twenty-five years in Iran he had never once been treated disrespectfully – either before the revolution or since.

We felt sad that the news media concentrated all their attention on what was happening outside the US Embassy. There was also much goodwill shown to us and to other foreigners. For instance, when eggs and milk got really short the shopkeepers would save some specially for Diana, knowing that we had two young children. Meat was also short. One day a local butcher, who suddenly had some meat, let Diana have as much as ten kilos of mince. She didn't have the money with her, but he told her to pay him another day. Diana's mother came to stay with us just at the time the Embassy was taken over. She was surprised to see how normally our daily life was able to continue.

Two weeks later she returned to England. We had our morning service in the church. Then there was a phone call from England. It was Diana's sister. Her father had been killed in a road accident the night before. We were stunned. Diana was overcome with tears, especially thinking of her mother who would be arriving at London airport in a few hours not knowing what had happened. The whole thing seemed hard to comprehend. We were the ones whose lives were at risk, yet he, in the comparative safety of England, had been killed. Within forty-eight hours Diana left with the children to join her mother for a month, and I stayed on to prepare for Christmas in the church.

It was a Christmas filled with deep meaning. Diana returned just in time for our family to be together again. The church was packed at our evening service, mostly with Iranians. I spoke from a verse in St John's Gospel:

'The light shines in the dark and the darkness does not put it out.'

Things did seem dark for the church. Who knew what might happen in the coming year?

As I was speaking I lit a candle and put out the lights. Except for the flame of that candle we were in total darkness.

'Does the darkness put out the flame?' I asked.

Of course it didn't. In fact that little flame seemed to glow all the brighter.

The evening before, a group of us had gathered in a house to sing carols. We were a mixture of Iranians, Americans and British. Despite the hostage situation we found ourselves united at a much deeper level in our common faith. I don't think any other group could have met in Teheran in this way – Iranians and Westerners together.

On New Year's Eve we decided reluctantly not to have a midnight service. It was becoming more dangerous to be out in the streets at night. We felt it was also important for the church to keep a low profile and not to draw too much attention to itself. The situation for foreigners was deteriorating. The British Embassy began to pack up and many of its staff left. The hostages were still held – though at that stage it was hoped their early release would be negotiated. Our own Embassy advised those who felt able to stick it out to do so, as there was real hope that things would improve.

Then there was a terrible air disaster to the north of the city. All 120 passengers were killed as their plane crashed into the mountains. It reminded me of another disaster, just a year before, when thousands were losing their lives in their fight against the Shah, and the earthquake at the desert town of Tabas killed many thousands more. Both times I felt the forces of nature were somehow caught up in the tragic mess of the country.

There were repeated demands by the government for the return of the Shah from Panama, with all his wealth. One day the headlines of the papers said that a deal had been negotiated and he was to be handed back. The car drivers in Teheran hooted their horns in jubilation, as was the custom at a time of celebration. But the rumour was false.

## Just like James Bond

All through those winter months a series of articles appeared in a weekly magazine. They were utterly untrue but could be read as fact by an undiscerning reader. They purported to reveal what I can only describe as the 'sex, sin and spying of the church', but their chief aim was to show the connection of our church with the CIA and British Intelligence.

Each week it read like a James Bond thriller! There were the midnight meetings, an attempted coup, coded letters, plots and counter-plots. But the names used were those of the missionaries, including our own, and Iranian Christians. In one of the articles it said that Diana had shot two Americans. The whole thing seemed ludicrous. We laughed at it, just because it was so far-fetched. But one day I talked about it with a taxi-driver and he asked me if any of it was true. Then we realized that others might be wondering about its truth as well.

We began to buy the magazine regularly and opened it with a certain amount of dread, not knowing what new lies would be splashed there for all to read. One week I was amazed to see printed in an article a letter which the British

Ambassador had written to me two months before. In fact it was the only letter I ever received from him – a short note reminding me that the Remembrance Day service was to be held at a certain time and that I was leading it – a totally harmless letter. The problem was this issue of the magazine carried a caption in Farsi:

'Letter of the British Ambassador written to the bishop.'

It was printed as evidence that we were spies because we had a link with the British Embassy. Because the readers didn't understand English they had no idea that the letter was not written to the bishop at all, and was quite innocuous.

I wondered how the writers of the articles had got hold of that letter. Was it an inside job at the Embassy? Or had someone broken into my study, taken the letter for photocopying and then returned it? (It was still in my possession.) Quite by chance I had kept the envelope in which the letter had been delivered by despatch rider. It was obvious that it had been opened, then re-sealed. Plainly it had been intercepted on its way from the Embassy, photocopied, and then delivered.

We still didn't think many people took the articles very seriously, but I got the feeling that as they continued week after week, for more than three months, those who wanted to make trouble for the church could use them as false evidence. So we became more apprehensive. What would the next article say? What new fable would it make up? Whose names would be used? Which photo would appear? The church, after much discussion, decided not to take any action, as any complaint could easily be twisted and thrown back in our face. The British Embassy did officially request the editor to deny the truth of the articles.

A new uncertainty came. To work in Iran, foreigners had always needed a work permit. Usually these were issued annually, but now when they expired they were not renewed.

Instead, an extension was given to each foreigner for two to three weeks. These would be issued until a final decision was made. So in February 1980 I began regular visits to the visa department to get an extension. Every few weeks my Iranian colleague and I would spend a whole morning visiting countless departments in a multi-storied building to get the precious extension recorded in the work permit.

## Fear

In the middle of the month, one of our church members was suddenly arrested and taken for questioning without warning. This was what we feared could happen to anybody at any moment. His wife rang me up late one evening and asked me to go and visit their family. I was glad to go, as they had welcomed my visits before. Others in the congregation had specifically asked me not to visit them in case it put them under suspicion of spying.

When I arrived I found them badly shaken by his sudden arrest. Some revolutionary guards had come and turned drawers and cupboards upside down, looking for anything that might be incriminating. And then they took him – his wife had no idea where. We sat and talked and prayed together. How long would they keep him? Would we see him again? How would they treat him? Before leaving, I read Jesus' words to his disciples, as they too faced so much uncertainty and fear:

'Peace I leave with you, my peace I give to you; not as the world gives do I give to you. Let not your hearts be troubled, neither let them be afraid.'

The following evening I visited them again. Still there was no news. Again we prayed and drew strength from the Bible.

On the third day news came that he had been released. I went to see him. There was a total blackout in the city; the electricity had failed as it often did. He lay on his bed, overcome with thankfulness to be free again. obviously he had been through a lot of questioning and faced something of an ordeal.

'But what an opportunity I had,' he told me. 'I explained the conversion of St Paul to the men who questioned me – they were really interested.'

As I sat with him I prayed the evening prayer from our Persian prayer book, translated from the English, which we used weekly in our worship. It seemed more relevant now than ever before:

'Lighten our darkness we beseech thee, O Lord, and defend us from all the perils and dangers of this night . . .'

Others too were living in fear. In one of the rooms next to my study worked one of the Iranian church staff. We would often have tea together in the middle of the morning and share our thoughts. He had much more to fear than I because he was an Iranian Christian convert. He was worried about his future and that of his family. He often came to work in dark glasses, and he varied the times he came and went, as well as the route he took. The curtain in his room was continually drawn so that he couldn't be seen from outside. At one point he discussed with me a possible escape route should anyone come to take us.

'Every time I hear footsteps in the corridor,' he said, 'I wonder if they've come for me.'

I found it was catching. I started hearing footsteps in the corridor too.

## Scarcity

Diana and I also discussed what the revolutionary guards would be after if they ever came to search our house. We didn't have any liquor, or articles or pictures to do with the Shah. We knew that often photo albums were taken as a good source of information against others. We put our family albums into a case, and Diana drove one morning, in thick snow, to a friend of ours, who promised to look after them for us.

One lunchtime I returned home half an hour later than usual. Someone had unexpectedly come to see me. Diana was very worried.

'I thought you'd either been shot or taken,' she said. 'I was about to come to the office – scared what I might find.'

After that we decided how important it was that I come back at the time arranged, or phone if I was delayed.

Another day the church administrator came up from Isfahan. He came into my study and immediately went to the window. Then he sat in my chair by my desk. I couldn't think what he was doing.

'You are safe,' he said. 'They can't shoot you from outside.'

I had never thought of anyone shooting me while I sat in my study, but he obviously spent much of his time thinking about his own safety and that of his family. And not without reason. In fact eventually he was imprisoned.

At that time too I asked my Iranian colleague to lock one of the offices in our corridor which had been left open by mistake. I told him I felt someone might come and steal something if we left it open. He misunderstood the way I had said this in Persian. He thought I said that someone was coming who would steal things! The result was that he spent the whole of that evening destroying all his day-to-day correspondence. He was gripped by fear.

A pastor from one of the other denominations told me one day he couldn't understand why a certain member of our church was so afraid. I tried to explain to him, but it was obvious he couldn't understand. Then it came to me – you only begin to understand fear when you are yourself in contact with those living with it all the time. This was something I was beginning to learn.

At the end of February the government announced a week they called 'general mobilization'. We wondered what this was all about. The order was given that no private car would go on the streets unless performing a public service. No reason was officially given except that this would help solve Teheran's traffic problems and it was more healthy to walk to work. But most people guessed the real reason was a lack of fuel because the vital pipelines in the south of the country had been sabotaged. The streets of Teheran were unbelievably empty. The taxis had a holiday!

On the Sunday of that week I thought no one would come to church. Most of the church members lived far away and would need to come by car. At least thirty were there, most of whom had spent several hours travelling by bus. Their worship meant a lot to them.

We made friends with an English girl married to an Iranian. They had been living in California and had recently returned to Iran with their one child. He had bought a small shop and was turning it into a restaurant. For them, as for us, eggs, meat and milk were getting scarce – sometimes unobtainable. One day we went to their little restaurant for a meal.

'You must regret coming back to Iran,' I said to them.

'On the contrary,' they replied, 'we much prefer it here to California. There life is all sex and money – no place to bring up a child. At least here a young person is given the opportunity to live a clean life, and it's worth all the shortages for that.'

## Darkness

In these months I found myself going through a period of darkness. I had deep fears that I tried to hide. What would the next article in that magazine say? Would the extension to the work permit be given? How much could I trust God for the safety of the family? Would I, as a pastor, be able to minister effectively to the Christians facing such pressures?

The words of the psalmist became part of my experience: 'Save me, O God, for the waters have come up to my neck ... I have come into deep waters, and the flood sweeps over me.'

After breakfast one day, when Rosemary had gone off to her play school and Deborah was keeping fairly quiet, Diana and I talked at some depth.

'I feel I'm making no progress in my spiritual life,' she said to me with real honesty. 'My love for God, the joy of life, seem to have gone.' I think it was more difficult for her than for me. At least in my job as pastor I had the duty to go into the church twice a day for prayer and for silence. She was a full-time mother with all the demands of young children. We worked it out together that for a time each day I would try to be with the children to let her go to church. This seemed to make a difference. In fact I could see the difference on her face when she returned after just half an hour alone with God in the church building. I reminded her too of some words which Margaret, a friend who worked with our missionary society, had spoken to us on our last leave in England.

'You can never judge your own spiritual growth,' she said. 'Go on being as faithful to God as you can. He will look after the rest.'

In retrospect we found we were learning far more than we realized at the time.

Meanwhile there were many encouragements. Some words our bishop had shared with us in Isfahan came back to me many times. He had visited a monastery in the Egyptian desert outside Cairo. A saintly old man, called Matthew the Poor, had said to him:

'When Islam seems to get stronger, that makes the church all the stronger too.'

I felt this was happening with us. The services continued to be well attended (even though one of the congregation had said to me when we first came that people would leave because I was a foreigner!). One family came straight from work on a Sunday evening and drove for an hour to get to the church. Another lady was so determined to come that she never told her Muslim husband (who wouldn't have permitted it). She told me her own father had been a Christian and that at all costs she must remain loyal. A young man from a Jewish family had become a Christian through the help of Iraj, the Iranian pastor. He never missed coming to church and was thrilled when I asked him to preach – a thing he had never done before.

One day after the service another member of the congregation, who helped me greatly with the preparation of sermons in Persian, told Diana she had received a vision of Christ:

'It was like the transfiguration of Jesus in the presence of his three disciples,' she said, 'he became so real to me.'

She was one who had to catch two or three buses each Sunday to get to church. Another man and his wife who lived twenty miles away came regularly:

'If we don't come we feel ill the following week,' she said.

They also started a regular prayer meeting in their own home.

## Blessing

One day a senior member of the church said to me:

'You know, this revolution has been the greatest blessing of my life to me.'

This staggered me. I knew he had lost a lot of money and some of his property.

'It was as if I'd come to a cul-de-sac in my life. I couldn't go forward any more; only God could help me out of it. I came to the end of myself, of my own resources. Then I learnt again that God loves me, that he calls me by my name, that I really matter to him. And then I began to know again the real meaning of joy and faith.'

He told me his first experience of God had happened thirty years before, when he walked alone in the streets of London, feeling empty and desolate.

'The love of God came and filled me – it was an overwhelming experience,' he said, 'and now I've been brought back to know his love for me again.'

Every Friday afternoon a group of young Iranian Christians met together. First we would play volleyball (their favourite game), and then have a time of reading the Bible and prayer, rounding off with tea together. One of them worked among students, quietly sharing her faith with them. Another was preparing for full membership of the church; he told me one day he would like to be ordained. Two of them were Christians studying at the university; they didn't know any other Christians there but neither wavered in their commitment to Christ. Another of them who often came was blind, but he found the way to our house through the crowded streets. Several times we united with youth groups from the Armenian and Assyrian churches. This gave great encouragement as we realized there were other young people remaining faithful.

Each month the Persian-speaking fellowship had a meeting. This started after the revolution. Farsi-speaking Christians from seven different churches came together. It was the first time meetings like this had ever been held.

'It takes a revolution to unite Christians,' I said to a friend.

'Perhaps we need one in Britain,' he replied.

Certainly we were beginning to grasp how little our differences matter compared to the unity we share in Christ.

Usually a speaker would talk on some subject, the identity of the Persian-speaking church, the history of the early church in Iran, ways and means of publishing Christian books; then there would be a time for open discussion.

On two or three days, when Iran as a country was facing bigger problems, the voice of the Ayatollah came over the radio, telling us all to go on to the roof tops of our houses at 8.45 p.m. and to shout out for a quarter of an hour:

'*Allah-o-Akbar, Allah-o-Akbar*' ('God is greater, God is greater').

We wondered if people would do this. Sure enough they did! From every roof top around us, and every open window, the familiar words echoed round the streets. In the face of mounting economic problems and shortages this was an effective way of bolstering the people's morale and preserving the unity of the country. It was the only time we ever heard our next-door neighbour's voice.

In early March came an important event in our church. A family of four were confirmed, so becoming full church members. This was a very rare happening in the history of our small church in Iran. Usually it was individuals who were baptized and confirmed; it was almost unheard of that a whole family be confirmed. They had been searching for something they didn't find in Islam. They looked elsewhere to find God and so began to come to church. Khalil, the previous pastor, had already baptized them. Weekly we met for instruction and prayer. Their presence was an enormous encouragement to the other Christians.

## No safe place

In Isfahan the situation was tense. The central church committee had met and specifically asked the bishop not to return. They felt that his life would be at risk, and it would only increase the danger to the church if he did return at this time. For the bishop this was a hard decision to accept. He wanted so much to return and lead the struggling church, but he respected their wishes, and decided not to return for the present.

Iraj, the priest in Isfahan, was one day approached by three men from the revolutionary council. He took them to his study. They questioned him for four hours about the church. When they asked him for the names of the members, he refused to give them.

'I am their shepherd,' he said, 'and the shepherd must guard his sheep.'

They never got the names from him.

Meanwhile his wife, Minoo, was in the house. She told me later how she began to pray for her husband.

'Three times I went on my knees in prayer,' she said, 'and then it was as if a voice told me to open the Bible. I opened it at the book of Zechariah, chapter 12.'

It was that chapter which spoke to her (she was a Christian from a Jewish background), and which brought her such comfort in her time of need. In it God promises to keep 'a watchful eye over his people', to be 'a shield to them', so that 'the feeblest among them will be like King David'.

'I was filled with a great peace,' she said. 'I was no longer afraid what they might do to Iraj.'

I was asked to attend a meeting of the central church committee in Isfahan and decided to go down by plane. It was a rather unusual, and at times hilarious journey! Another Iranian member of the committee, whom I knew well, was also attending the meeting. He was very concerned that on the journey he should not be seen with a foreigner, in case he was suspected of spying. So we agreed not to travel together. We said goodbye to each other before entering the departure

Bahram, only son of Bishop Dehqani-Tafti and Margaret, killed in Teheran on 6 May 1980.

lounge at the airport. Waiting for the plane, we sat well apart. I delayed joining the queue to board the plane until the very last, only to find that he had done the same. Once on board he was sitting two rows in front of me. All seemed to be going well until the steward asked to see his ticket.

'You are in the wrong seat, sir,' he said, and asked him to move two rows back.

That meant he was sitting next to me! We didn't utter a word to each other on the forty-five minute flight. When we disembarked we still didn't communicate. We had decided to take different taxis to the church. Imagine my feelings when the driver of my taxi slowed down to pick up my friend a little further down the road! For some reason the driver suddenly decided not to stop, so we did arrive separately at the meeting, as arranged.

Another of our anxieties in these months was that the money in the church central fund would be seized. Nearly everything had by now been illegally taken over. Only this fund, the church buildings, and the blind school for girls remained. The central accounts and ledger books had also not been taken. These were vital, as we still had to pay the wages of different people working for the church. But where should we keep them? Where would they be safe? One whole evening I drove the financial accountant round Teheran in my car. We didn't know a safe place for those ledgers. We thought of various homes, and visited two of them. But we knew that if they were found it could mean trouble for those living there. Ultimately we did find a relatively safe place. But within a few months the accountant's house was ransacked, and the central fund was taken over as well. Nowhere was safe.

One afternoon the bell rang and I opened the door. There stood the Papal Nuncio, the Pope's personal representative in Teheran. He was a big, round man who instantly put his friendly arm round me and led me into the sitting-room. I didn't know any Italian, but in rather broken English he was able to explain that there had been a threat to take over the Bishop Thompson chapel (which belonged to our church) in Isfahan, and to turn it into a mosque.

'This threatens all the churches in Iran,' he said.

Apparently Iraj in Isfahan had tried to contact me but without success, so he got in touch with the Papal Nuncio. This was disquieting news. Until now no church buildings had been touched. The Nuncio said that the Armenian archbishop was also very concerned at this news.

'If you are in difficulty please contact me immediately,' he said.

In fact the threat, through a phone call, was not immediately followed up, and it was only some months later that the chapel was taken over and turned into a mosque.

## Farsi funeral

The Persian New Year came on 21 March. Like the Iranians we went out for a celebration picnic. We met some friends by the gate of the church and stopped to talk. As we got into the car, we thoughtlessly left the baby's push-chair and other valuable belongings standing by the door. I remembered twenty minutes later and we returned, hoping against hope they would still be there. They had all disappeared. We felt angry with ourselves for our forgetfulness. The next morning the door bell rang. A little lady in a black chadoor stood there holding the push-chair and all the other things we had left behind.

'I saw them yesterday,' she said, 'and thought I'd look after them for you.'

I wondered if that would have happened back home.

In April the business of the work permits still made us unsettled. Suddenly I was given one for three months. This at least looked more promising. Or perhaps they'd just got fed up with my regular visits.

Law and order seemed to be further deteriorating. The home of one of our church members was burgled. The streets were filled with unemployed young men, trying to sell cigarettes and balloons. Big demonstrations were held against America and Iraq. I listened each week to the sermon preached at the Friday prayers at the university. It was always broadcast on radio and television. For Muslims, religion and politics are closely linked, so the sermons were as much about politics as religion. Mrs Thatcher's name often came up, and her policies came in for criticism. So of course did the name of President Carter, to them 'the greatest Satan of them all'. The streets around the university would be packed as the message was relayed to the masses sitting in the roads. But in the university itself there was continual unrest, as left-wing groups opposed the religious fundamentalists.

Meanwhile daily there was fighting in Kurdestan, with much loss of life. There was talk of the complete closure of the British Embassy to support President Carter's economic sanctions. The Embassy staff began to leave.

'We seem to have been through all this before,' I said to my friend from the British Council.

He had been chairman of the British security committee in Isfahan just over a year before.

Our own family life was uncertain. Diana used to discuss with a recently-arrived English friend whether she was putting up pictures in her house or taking them down! Our routine continued, but Diana often said she wondered if we would stay there long enough to eat the food she'd bought that day. It was difficult to know whether to build food stocks up because of shortages (of eggs, meat and milk) or to let them run down as we might be leaving soon.

In the middle of April a member of our Persian church

died. He was a man of real faith. Just the week before, despite having suffered three heart attacks, he had been brought to church and received holy communion. The funeral arrangements seemed so complicated, especially as I had to do it all in Farsi. First no one knew where the books for a funeral service were kept. After much searching I found some in the bottom of an old cupboard and quickly did my homework so that I could take it in Farsi. Then we had to arrange to get the body out of the hospital. The paperwork involved seemed never-ending, and I waited in the hospital for what seemed like hours before finally the permission was given. Then nobody was willing to lift the corpse into the coffin – to Muslims a Christian body is unclean. I found one other person willing to help me do this, but it needed all our strength. Fifty people stood round watching us struggle.

I told the driver of the car carrying the coffin not to go too fast in the Teheran traffic, as I didn't know the precise route to the cemetery and wanted to follow him. He promised not to, but didn't keep his promise. I did lose him, and also lost the way in the maze of streets. I had visions of the family waiting for me to arrive and losing all their patience. In desperation I stopped two young men in the street, Mohammed and Reza, and asked them to get into the car to show me the way. We arrived and fortunately not all the family had got there before us. Then there was the question of who should clean the body.

'That's the job of the priest,' they said.

I felt it wasn't my job at all!

In the end we found a compromise, and the service did take place. I found myself hoping desperately that no one else in the congregation would die!

Afterwards I talked with one of the dead man's family. He told me he was a secret Christian believer.

'You know,' he said, 'a Muslim who becomes a Christian must be killed.'

## Great Satan

A few days later the Americans made their abortive attempt to rescue the hostages. What a debacle in the desert it was, with the helicopters caught in the sand storms, two of them colliding and the others flying away, leaving dead bodies in the sand. The anger of the Iranians was immense. They were convinced that America had planned to take the airport and invade the country.

'God is on our side,' an Iranian said to me triumphantly as I bought a newspaper. 'Now we know we are in the right.'

'The Great Satan' was made to look even more sinister.

Our reactions were mixed. We longed for the release of the hostages. Who could know all that they had been through? But we also knew that if the plan had worked the life of every foreigner in Iran would have been in danger. As it was, the lives of the hostages remained intact, and so did ours.

The following Sunday I asked the members of our Persian church committee to meet with me before the evening service. I wanted their reassurance that they were still happy to have me, a foreigner, as their pastor. I thought perhaps I was becoming an embarrassment to them. We had a frank discussion. They were surprised I should even have thought of leaving. Unanimously they asked us to remain. The words of the sermon, preached by a member of the congregation who was himself later to be imprisoned, spoke deeply to many of us there. He spoke on the words of Jesus:

'Let not your hearts be troubled. You believe in God. Believe also in me.'

Two days later I went to Isfahan to attend another meeting of the church central committee. Although I didn't know it, this was to be my last visit. I walked up to the theological college in the main street, the place to which I had so often gone for silence and reflection. The doors were closely barred. It was no longer open to outsiders. The gateman, whom I knew well, drew me to one side and whispered in my ear:

'Everything is dying.'

Sadly I returned to Iraj's house. Several committee members had gathered. We exchanged greetings, and then went by separate ways, at intervals of a few minutes, to the room where the meeting was to be held. It was important to keep a low profile. No one knew who might be watching.

I returned by bus to Teheran the next day. It was to be my last view of the desert. The journey took several hours, all of it through that familiar wasteland. There it was, empty and vast, with little pockets of snow sparkling in the sun on the mountain tops. The sheep and goats faithfully followed the shepherd to find pasture. Villagers stood round a well, with its big wheel, drawing up the water. The young man sitting next to me told me he was leaving city life to go back to working on the land. The little group near me in the bus asked countless questions about my job and family. There were no secrets on these bus journeys!

## Be still

As I entered the flat Diana told me the news that the Iranian Embassy in London had been seized by guerrillas. It really did seem that anything could happen. We knew that the fate of that Embassy and our own were bound together. It could so easily have created yet stronger anti-British feeling.

The following day was May Day. For us the storm reached its height. Those two young gunmen I described in the first chapter entered our building. Jean Waddell was shot. Yet her life, and ours, were miraculously preserved.

Diana was shut in that bathroom with the two children, utterly defenceless. The gunmen could be anywhere – and about to do anything.

'Tell me a story,' said Rosemary.

'What story shall I tell you?' asked Diana.

'The story of the storm,' said the three-year-old.

So she began to tell the so-familiar story. There was the storm on the sea. Jesus was lying asleep at the end of the boat. The waves got bigger. The wind blew stronger. The little boat began filling with water. It looked as if they would all sink. But Jesus was still asleep. His friends woke him up.

'Don't you care if we drown?' they shouted.

Jesus got up. He said to the wind:

'Be quiet!'

And to the waves:

'Be still!'

Then he said to his friends:

'Why were you afraid? Didn't you know that I was with you?'

At that moment the reality of the story was so great, it was as though God was saying to Diana those very words.

'Don't be afraid. I am with you. Not a hair on your head will be touched.'

It was in the storm that those disciples began to experience the power of Christ's presence. That day, and particularly for Diana in the bathroom, we felt nearer to Christ than ever before. I wrote in my diary some words from the Bible:

'Surely God is in this place and we knew it not.'

A Persian hymn puts it like this:

'It is stormy on the sea of life,
But I do not fear, because you are there.'

# 10
# SURE AND CERTAIN HOPE

It was mid-afternoon of 6 May. The phone rang. Margaret Dehqani was speaking from the hospital where she was looking after Jean Waddell (Jean had been shot just five days before). Her voice was anxious. She was speaking about her twenty-four-year-old son.

'Please pray for Bahram,' she said. 'He should have come here two hours ago but he hasn't arrived. I have a feeling something has happened to him and I wanted to ask for your prayers.'

I think it was about three hours later when she phoned again:

'I've heard Bahram has had some kind of accident but he's all right. Please pray for him.'

We wondered just what had happened, and prayed.

About 9 p.m. a phone call came from the Intercontinental Hotel. That was where Bahram was doing part-time work as an interpreter for the American NBC news. One of his colleagues was speaking.

'I have difficult news to tell you,' he said. 'It's about Bahram . . . he's been shot . . . he's dead.'

Briefly he told me the bare facts as he knew them. Bahram's car had been cornered on a northern highway in Teheran near Evin prison. He'd been forced to stop. He'd been shot while still in the car.

'We want you to go and tell his mother,' he continued. 'I'm sorry to give you this awful job to do.'

I spluttered my thanks and put the receiver down in tears.

It all seemed so impossible. Just the night before he was with us in our flat. We went upstairs together to Jean's flat to look at her bed. He wanted to find the bullet mark. We found it in the sheet on her bed. There was no doubt that she'd been shot in cold blood, rather than in the struggle beforehand. He was then on his way to see his mother and Jean in hospital. As he left the flat I asked him to thank the two police guards downstairs for all they were doing to protect our lives. He gladly did this. It was a way of encouraging them not to get too slack. Then he had gone – and now his life was finished.

**Given back**

I was reluctant to leave Diana alone in the flat with the children, despite the police guards. Also, we had decided it would be foolish for me to go out alone, as we knew my life was at risk. I phoned Ned Barret at the Embassy. He said he would be over right away and bring Tricia, who could be released from her work at the Embassy to look after Jean in hospital. This would leave Margaret free to come away and spend the night at our house. We waited an hour, but it seemed much longer. Still they hadn't arrived. They must have lost their way, we thought. It was getting late. We agreed I should go on alone and see Margaret.

It wasn't easy waiting at the hospital reception desk while they called her to come down.

'What do I say? How do I say it?'

Then she came. Instinctively she knew that something was wrong. I took her to the corner of the room and we sat down. I knew I had to break it very slowly, to cushion the terrible shock.

'I have some difficult news to tell you, Margaret,' I said. 'It's bad news ... it's not easy for me to say it ... it's about Bahram.'

'Have they killed him?' she asked (or something like that).

'Yes.'

'Do you know how it happened?'

I told her all I knew.

There seemed no more words to say. They had dried up. Tears and a deep sigh of grief gripped her. Then she did manage to speak.

'God gave him to us ... we give him back to God,' is the sentence I remember.

A nurse brought us some tissues. We must have sat there for about twenty minutes.

After that, we went up to Jean's room and told her what had happened.

'The news of his death came as a dreadful shock,' she wrote later. 'I just couldn't get past the actual words "Bahram's been shot". I couldn't feel anything, but Margaret was wonderful ...'

Margaret had nursed Jean back into a much stronger condition by constant care and encouragement. Now it was Jean who was able to bring some comfort to her while I returned to our flat to collect Tricia.

Finally Margaret was able to leave the hospital and come to our flat. Diana tried repeatedly to phone London but, although by now it was 1 a.m., all the lines were engaged. Finally we got through. Margaret spoke with her sister and brother-in-law in London. They had just recently suffered the tragic death of their only son, Paul, in a drowning accident. I doubt if those two sisters had ever been closer to each other than in that moment. It was so frustrating that she couldn't contact her husband direct, as there was no telephone line to Cyprus where he was attending a conference.

From London they managed to get through to the bishop in Cyprus. How he must have longed to be with Margaret. It seemed clear that they had taken Bahram's life because they couldn't get at the bishop. The following day a telegram arrived from him. He quoted one of the psalms:

> 'Have mercy on me, O God,
> Have mercy on me,
> For in you my soul takes refuge.
> I will take refuge in the shadow of your wings
> Until the disaster has passed . . .'

These words seemed to say all that could be said.

The following morning I drove Margaret and two of her close Persian friends to Bahram's flat. We heard from the doorman that he had gone there the night before (presumably after leaving the hospital) and apparently those who wanted to kill him had tried to enter his house through the roof. They had cut off the lights. But Bahram managed to escape. I saw a book which I had lent him lying by his bedside. Its title was *Freedom in the modern world.* This was why he decided to stay in his own country, I thought. He wanted to find his freedom among his own people. How much they had misunderstood him.

We drove up to the north of the city, to the hospital where his body was being held. The car which Bahram had been driving was there. We saw a bullet hole in the roof and his blood on the seat. We pieced together more clearly what had happened. It seemed that another car had overtaken him and then forced him off the road. One of the men from the car got in with Bahram and at gunpoint told him to drive on. If the man had threatened to kill him, there would have been some struggle. As it was, it appears they drove on for a while and stopped in a lonely place. A boy who passed said he saw them talking together and then heard a gunshot. From Bahram's body it was evident that he hadn't struggled. Presumably he didn't know they would shoot him. The other car then got away.

## People matter

At the police station they produced the briefcase that had been in his car. They took down details about his life. My mind kept going back to that afternoon he and I had spent together a few weeks before. He played the organ in the church and came back for lunch. We spent the afternoon talking. Although I'd known him for several years, this was the first time we really got talking in depth.

In some ways he and I came from similar backgrounds. Our parents were deeply committed Christians. We'd gone to the same boarding school in the west of England which was known for its Christian tradition. I'd already struggled to find the reality of God for myself, apart from my family and background. Now he was going through the same kind of search.

'I've got to stand aside a bit,' he said to me, 'and this means people misunderstand me. But it's the only way I can truly be myself.'

The title of the book by his bedside seemed so relevant: *Freedom in the modern world.*

In that conversation he was very realistic about the church.

'The church needs this revolution,' he told me quite bluntly.

I couldn't understand what he meant. How could a revolution be necessary for a small, struggling body of people trying to hold to what they believe is true? All that the world could see were the things the church had lost – the bishop in virtual exile, the senior pastor murdered, the lives of the others threatened, the institutions seized, the funds in jeopardy.

'But don't you see?' he said. 'The problem with the church is that it's too concerned with buildings and property. The important thing is people. The church must come back to seeing the importance of people.'

When a BBC interviewer talked with us a few days later I told him what Bahram had said.

'Isn't that something the church in England has to learn as well?' he remarked.

I sat looking at the briefcase in that police station. I had last seen it as Bahram sat at the organ in our church when he'd played at our Good Friday service just a month before. His death seemed so utterly pointless.

The next morning I went down into the church cellars to find a coffin. The caretaker helped me carry it upstairs. Two young Christian men from Shiraz had driven up that night. They came to collect it and take it to the hospital. They took Bahram's body to Isfahan, and Margaret, with Shireen and Guli, her two daughters, followed in another car.

## God, forgive

That evening an Iranian girl in her late teens, one of Bahram's students at the college where he taught, came to our flat with her mother. When we opened the door they stumbled in both sobbing with grief. She asked lots of questions and kept on saying, '*Khoda neest*' ('There is no God'). Her anger against God (Bahram's God), against the church, against us, poured out of her.

What could we say? We held her and tried to bring some comfort. We too felt something of her anger. Why had God allowed this? Where was he in all this?

That girl went down to Isfahan next day for Bahram's funeral service. I wasn't able to go, as we had a service in our church, but the Roman Catholic archbishop went to represent the churches in Teheran. On his return he told us what a moving service it had been. Iraj, the priest, asked Margaret to say a few words about her son. She stood next to the coffin. At one point she held on to it for support.

'He gave his life for his father,' she said in Persian. 'We believe that God will transform this evil and meaningless act and make it a blessing and use it for the strengthening of his church.'

She repeated the words of Jesus on the cross:

'Father, forgive them, they know not what they do.'

In her prayer she said:

'O God, forgive our enemies and those who are evil to us, and do not allow a spirit of revenge and hatred to remain in us.'

I feel sure that it was those words, and the witness of that service to the resurrection of Christ, that changed the life of that Iranian girl. I met her again ten days later at the memorial service we held for Bahram in our church in Teheran. She came up to me after the service.

'*Khoda hast*' ('There is God'), she said. 'Bahram's death has shown him to me.'

Behind her tears her face had softened. The anger and the despair had lifted. The spirit of Bahram still lived. He had been the means of bringing her to God.

Another Iranian later put it this way:

'The tears that have flowed have washed away the cobwebs in our faith.'

'The church is people,' Bahram had said. I've often thought of those words. Your possessions, your freedom, your family, can all be taken from you. But who can take away a person's inner being? Who can take away your faith?

I think of an elderly bedridden lady, Rogiyeh, in a village just outside Isfahan. We went to visit her several times. She lay on a mattress on the floor, and we sat round it with our feet under the warm *korsee* (a charcoal fire enclosed in a container with a blanket on it) and sipped tea. Her face had a deep joy as she told us her story.

About thirty years before she fell from a tree, though

miraculously her pregnancy was not affected. Her child was born but she herself was paralyzed. Her husband left her. The hospital staff did all they could for her but finally she was discharged as they couldn't help her physically. In her own home one night she had a dream and saw Jesus Christ. He commanded her to get up and walk, and she was healed. When she woke she obeyed the dream command. With the aid of two sticks, and to the amazement of her doctors, she was able to walk again.

This was the turning-point of her life. She gave herself to Christ and for many years became the evangelist at the hospital. Now she was lying helpless. And yet, as Margaret Dehqani said as we left Rogiyeh's house one day:

'I always leave her a fuller person than when I went.'

Yes, it's people that matter – people and their faith.

## Shared vision

A young student doctor sat with me in my study in Teheran. His face was kind and sensitive, but he was restless as he talked and I knew he was rootless too.

In Isfahan he had studied at the university and we'd often talked together. I remember some tapes we listened to, which showed us the way modern psychiatry can help us understand the Christian faith. We talked about Marxism, which he had studied at some depth. He felt we had a lot to learn from it. We discussed the revolution too. At about the time of one of our conversations, it was made compulsory for women to wear the *chadoor*; many women were marching in the streets of Teheran, fighting for the right not to wear it.

'The revolution has lost its direction,' he said to me.

He was searching for something stable and real for his own life.

In Teheran, where he had come to do further medical studies, he occasionally came to church. He took the Bible reading at our daughter Deborah's baptism service. He occasionally joined the young people's group on Friday afternoons. Quite often he talked about his own baptism and asked me if I would baptize him with his mother. Then we lost touch with each other, until that afternoon.

'The problem is,' he said, 'that if I become a Christian I lose my identity with my people. I'll be cut off from my fellow countrymen. I need to find myself. I can't do it if I become a Christian.'

As we talked I could sense the agony he faced. He felt the pull of Christ, but he felt deep within him his own identity with his people, most of whom were Muslims.

'Who am I really?' he asked me.

This I knew was the inner struggle of every Iranian who wished to change his faith. Bishop Dehqani had always said of himself that in becoming a Christian he had remained just as truly a Persian. He had kept his Persian name, Hassan, as a sign of this. His allegiance to Christ never lessened his loyalty to his country and to his culture. Yet each one had to find this out for himself. This young man was caught in the same dilemma.

He told me he felt the church had lost touch with the poor and the oppressed.

'It is among them that I must find God,' he said.

I didn't try to argue with him, although I could have pointed out all our small church had done for the blind, for the sick and for those who needed hostels because they couldn't afford to live elsewhere.

'Three times a week I go to the tin shanty towns in the south of Teheran with my medical professor from the university, and we help the sick,' he told me.

We said farewell. I felt I might not see him again. Yet he too, in a different way, shared Bahram's vision – it's people who matter.

## Worth it?

We found much uncertainty in those last weeks. We knew some people wanted to kill us. We didn't know if we could get an exit visa to leave the country. We didn't know who in the church might be the next object of attack. I drew strength from a last meeting we had in Isfahan, just two days before Jean was shot.

When we met that time none of us knew that four out of the seven and the wife of another would be imprisoned, and three of us would be able to leave the country with our lives intact. The meeting was led by Iraj, the Isfahani pastor. Others who were there included Margaret Dehqani, Nosrattullah Sharifian, who was pastor in Kerman, Demetri Belos, the church administrator, and Dr John Coleman.

As it was just three weeks after Easter Day we looked together at the story of the disciples after Jesus' resurrection. They had gone back to their fishing on the sea of Galilee. They were in difficulties. All night they had been fishing and had caught nothing.

'They were disillusioned,' said Iraj. 'It was as if the resurrection had made no difference to their lives. And then they saw Jesus. There he was standing on the shore . . . he was there, with them – as he is with us – in every difficulty.'

One short sentence he used struck me forcibly:

'Faith alone is sufficient when everything else fails.'

Those words were to be more true than he could ever have imagined. Within a short time he was taken and imprisoned.

Another sentence I wrote down:

'We need difficulties to open our eyes.'

How true this was for us at this time.

That was the last time I saw Nosrattullah, the pastor from Kerman (a big city in the south-east of Iran). At this meeting he told us how his church property had been used as a polling booth for the voting in the recent elections. He was glad it had been chosen because it showed the church was respected and he was trusted. He told us too that, after five years of friendship with a young man, he had prepared him for baptism and finally had decided it was right to baptize him.

'It was a great witness for Christ,' he said.

I had worked for eighteen months with Nosrattullah when we first arrived in Isfahan. He was pastor to the church there before he moved to Kerman. We met together each week for tea and discussion. Once he told me how he became a Christian. It was when he worked in a factory in Isfahan. He had a friend called Hassan who was a Christian. One day over a hundred men from the factory took Hassan outside and beat him, telling him to renounce his faith. He refused. Nosrattullah was so impressed by his courage that he turned to Christ. His family, particularly his three brothers, were very angry when they heard what he had done and turned him out of the house. He went to live on Mount Sufeh (where he often joined us for the mountain walk), as he hadn't anywhere else to go. Later he felt God calling him to be ordained.

A few months before this meeting in Isfahan he had preached at Dr John Coleman's ordination. He used words from the same chapter we studied that evening:

'Jesus said: "Simon, son of John, do you love me more than anything else?"'

These words became real to me in a new way when I heard that, at the end of August 1980, Nosrattullah had been imprisoned.

That meeting was also the last time I talked with Demetri Belos, the church administrator. He too was imprisoned just over three months afterwards. A few weeks before, I had driven with him in his car in Teheran. He turned to me and said:

Dr John Coleman and his wife Audrey. John worked as a doctor in the city of Yazd. They were later imprisoned, and their whereabouts remained unknown for several months.

'Is it all worth it?'

He was talking about the risk of being a Christian. Sometimes the cost of his commitment was only too clear.

## Imprisonment

In those last three weeks we had a twenty-four-hour police guard at our front door. I didn't go out alone for fear of being shot. But we still had to make those visits to try and get an exit visa. My Iranian colleague always came with me.

We were all very worried about the three remaining missionaries in Isfahan, Margaret, Libby and Anne. Was it right for them to stay? How safe were they? What would happen to the girls' blind school if they left? In the end the church felt it was safe and right for them to stay. But in fact a few weeks later they were ordered by the Government to leave the country within seventy-two hours. At least their lives were intact. Meanwhile we began to sell what we could of our belongings, and to pack up, in the hope of getting the visa.

John and Audrey Coleman came to visit us. They were passing through Teheran on their way back to Yazd where John had been quietly continuing his medical work for the past two years. Each day fifty to seventy patients came to the clinic for medical treatment. Often he would go out into the villages and visit the sick. He was greatly respected and well liked. I got to know him in a special way, as the bishop asked me to prepare him for ordination. It was felt he would be a tremendous help in the church if he was ordained. He worked very hard to prepare for this, on top of all his work in the clinic and the villages. He wrote twenty-five essays on topics to do with the Bible and the church. Now that he was ordained he could take the service of holy communion, not only in Yazd but also in Shiraz and other churches.

Their situation in Yazd was rather a lonely one. There

were no other Westerners there. The English-speaking service was attended by Indians and Pakistanis. Only three or four came to the Persian service. Audrey would quite often phone Diana so that she could speak to someone in her own language.

As we said goodbye, I said to John:

'At least in Yazd you won't have any trouble.'

He agreed. But we had seriously underestimated the opposition to the church. Within three months they had both been summoned to Teheran and detained there.

Meanwhile Jean was out of hospital and recovering well from her gunshot wound and from all the emotional suffering she had been through. We saw her regularly. She had no bitterness against those who had shot her, although she was naturally afraid in case they tried to get her again.

She wrote this soon afterwards:

'It's comparatively easy for me to feel pity for my two gunmen; they seemed such ordinary boys but putting all their faith in their guns. We don't know what may have happened to them in their short lives to make them do what they did to me.'

It was obvious to us how full of gratitude she was for the strength she had been given to come through her ordeal. Her love for the Iranians seemed just as great. She also wrote:

'Always I am led back to the Sermon on the Mount, particularly the words of Jesus: "Love your enemies, do good to them that hate you". We are seeing the reaction of Iranian people to so much that they have had to suffer over the years from both inside and outside their country. They feel they have been manipulated by the big powers and made helpless to decide their own destiny. Now they are fiercely independent.

One night in those three weeks there was a blackout. The electricity in the city failed again. Rosemary, our three-year-old, woke up and wanted to go to the bathroom. Her words, as she took my hand down the corridor, feeling our way together through the dark, seemed to sum up so much that we were experiencing.

'I can't see Jesus ... but I follow him ... He's with us in the dark, and in the light.'

We had mixed feelings as we continued the packing and tried to keep life as normal as we could for the sake of the children. Rosemary still went to playschool; the police guard watched Diana wave her off each time. Diana never went out alone. We ate up our stores and others brought us milk. But we were pulled in two directions. We knew it was right to go. In fact the committee of the Persian church had now asked us to leave. And yet it seemed so hard to leave others behind, especially the church members. In a strange way we felt we had received far more than anything we might have given.

'You know,' said Diana, 'I can't say it's done Iran any good spiritually that I've been here, but I know I'm infinitely richer for being able to stay for as long as we have.'

In quite a new way God had become real to us.

## Hope

By the time of Bahram's memorial service we were ready to leave. That precious exit visa had been obtained. Over 700 people attended the service, most of them Muslims.

Iraj preached. He thanked God for Bahram's life, for his many talents and gifts, for him as a person. Then he spoke of the meaning of suffering. You could hear a pin drop. He pointed to the way suffering could transform the power of evil. He talked about the open hands of Jesus on the cross, stretched out, and reaching to the world.

'Christ took the sufferings of the world on himself and released a new power of love and forgiveness,' he said.

Before we left the country, I asked the Roman Catholic archbishop:

'Why is it that our Anglican church in Iran has suffered so much?'

'Yours is the church that has made the converts,' he replied.

This was certainly one of the two main reasons. The church was small but many of its members were converts from another faith – Islam, Judaism, or Zoroastrianism (the ancient Iranian religion). It had always shown great respect for Islam and tried to find areas of common agreement and concern. But there was no way round the fact that, to a Muslim, conversion to another faith was a betrayal and grounds for death. One Muslim convert told us how, when he became a Christian, his family held a burial service for him. He was more fortunate than some.

The other reason is because the church stood up and opposed every illegal act that took place against it, refusing to give in. Whether it was the murder of the senior pastor, or the take-over of the hospitals, or the confiscation of the schools, protest was made every time in the name of justice to the highest authorities in the country. Also none of the church money was handed over, despite constant demands. This angered those who thought the church would give in and not have the courage to protest.

The result was that some people forged documents against the church and accused its members of being spies. The fact that there was a fairly large number of foreign missionaries was used by such people as evidence of the link between the church and the Western spy network.

For the institutions to be run, a large number of foreign Christians came as workers, and this reliance on Westerners can leave the church open to all sorts of misunderstanding. For an Iranian nothing is quite as it appears on the surface. And so they found it difficult to accept that missionaries were there simply to do their work – as doctors, teachers, and so on

– and to share their love of Christ. There must be another reason, some thought. What could this be? Perhaps we were spies. We know there is no truth whatever in this, yet there is just no convincing those who are sure we have other motives. Those who want to attack the church can all too easily (though falsely) accuse it of being politically involved with the West.

At this time it looked as if everything was disintegrating. The church looked so vulnerable. So much had been lost. But we knew this was not the whole truth. The very difficulties were the means of strengthening the faith of the Christians. There was death. And yet Christians were finding that God was greater even than this.

As I said goodbye to Iraj on the evening before we left Iran his last words were: 'He is risen.' That is the source of all our hope.

In the words of Bishop Dehqani:

'Never before have we been so optimistic about the future of the church in our land as we are now. Our numbers have become smaller, our earthly supports have gone, but we are learning the meaning of faith in a new and deeper way.'

# POSTSCRIPT

On 21 May 1980, Diana, Rosemary, Deborah and I flew out of Mehrabod airport, Teheran to Bahrein in the Gulf. There we stayed for three weeks, recuperating with friends. Then, on 10 June, we flew into Heathrow airport, London.

Two months followed in Iran of great uncertainty, but without any major disasters. It was a time during which various political developments took place in the country. But August 1980 proved a terrible month for the Christians. A diary for the middle two weeks of that month would read like this:

5 August – Jean Waddell summoned from Teheran to Isfahan and arrested.

9 – Demetri Belos, church administrator, arrested in Teheran.

9– Margaret, Libby and Anne expelled from girls' blind school, 'Noor Ayin', in Isfahan, and told to leave the country.

10 – Dr John Coleman and his wife Audrey summoned from Yazd to Teheran and arrested.

17 – The Rev. Iraj Muttahedeh arrested in Isfahan.

20 – The Rev. Nosrattullah Sharifian arrested in Kerman.

Other members of the church were arrested too. Some were later released, but not all.

After long months of diplomatic activity, the American

hostages were released in January 1981. Then we had the news that Jean, John and Audrey would be freed, together with businessman Andrew Pike.

Even with the British prisoners released, the Christians in Iran will still have to face the storms. But all the signs are that they will come out the stronger. One of our church members in Teheran released a message from his prison saying how his experience, far from weakening his faith, had immeasurably strengthened it.

'My life will never be the same again,' he said.

He had found 'the deeper way'.

I often remember the words another Iranian said to me after being arrested and then released: 'We must never take our eyes off Mount Damarvand (Iran's highest mountain).'

I knew what he meant. The top of that snow-capped summit is a kind of symbol of the glory of Christ himself.

That man, even now, sits with his family in St Pauls church, Teheran each Sunday evening . . .